Praise for P|

MW00639583

"Do you think of your slide presentations as documentaries? Do you know how to highlight and spotlight key information on your slides using the "shapes" tool? Do you know when to abandon slides altogether? If not, then you need Norman Eng's *PRESENTING. The Professor's Guide to Powerful Communication*, your one-stop shop for creating dynamic, professional-level presentations for any kind of audience, whether students, colleagues, or laypeople. You'll learn how to implement the organization, interaction, and design principles that cognitive psychology and multimedia research endorse, all while enjoying Eng's crisp, concise writing, plentiful cross-disciplinary examples, and engaging visuals and videos."
—**LINDA B. NILSON**, Director Emeritus, Office of Teaching Effectiveness and Innovation, Clemson University, and author of *Teaching at Its Best*

"For all of us who have wrestled with the finer points of doing presentations, both with and without PowerPoint, Dr. Eng's *PRESENTING.* is a revelation. Cutting to the core of essential considerations for creating presentations and supplemented by a myriad of excellent tips and specific guidance, the book stands out as an eminently usable, readable and encouraging work. I highly recommend *PRESENTING* for those making presentations on a regular basis."
—**BRUCE ROSENBLOOM,** Director of the Center for Excellence in Teaching and Learning, City College of New York/CUNY

"Whether a professor is presenting to students, colleagues, or others, Dr. Eng offers powerful tips to make the time impactful. This book is an enjoyable read that is packed with pro tips and rich in resources, while still being a concise read. Professors (and their audiences!) will benefit tremendously from this powerful book."
—**JENNY GRANT RANKIN**, Lecturer and Author of *Sharing Your Education Expertise with the World: Make Research Resonate and Widen Your Impact*

"A quick read with exceptional content. Within higher education, over the past 20 years there has been a strong move from 'teaching' to 'learning.' In that time, we have focused on student outcomes and seem to have forgotten to note that the way we present information to learners has a tremendous impact on their ability to learn. In *PRESENTING: The Professor's Guide to Powerful Communication*, Dr. Eng both reminds us, and shows us, how we can deliver more impactful presentations. The bottom line is that as faculty, if we are going to spend the time amassing content to help students learn, we should be mindful of how that information is presented in ways that maximize their learning. This book does that."
—**TODD ZAKRAJSEK**, Associate Director, Faculty Development Fellowship, UNC-Chapel Hill, Director, Lilly Conferences, and co-author, *Teaching for Learning*, *The New Science of Learning*, and *Dynamic Lecturing*.

Also by Norman Eng

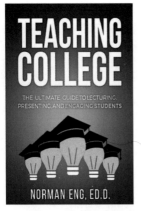

Available in ebook, paperback, and audiobook format

Available in ebook format only

NormanEng.org/books

Praise for *Teaching College*

"Fairly new to teaching? Pressed for time? Then *Teaching College* is the shortest distance between fear and success. It's easy to read, peppered with great tips, action steps, and illustrative videos, and brimming with ways to make your course and course materials personally relevant and interesting to your students."
—**LINDA B. NILSON**, Director Emeritus, Office of Teaching Effectiveness and Innovation, Clemson University, and author of *Teaching at Its Best*

"Dr. Eng tackles one of the biggest problems facing higher education: so few professors are adept at the art of teaching. Dr. Eng provides sound strategies for improving professors' communication of ideas, student engagement, and actual student learning. I found the writing style to be both inviting and enjoyable. This is a 'must read' for any professor who cares whether or not his or her students benefit from class."
—**JENNY GRANT RANKIN**, TEDx speaker, award-winning educator, and lecturer, University of Cambridge, UK.

"A really useful book for any college professor who wants to move beyond lectures and give students deeper engagement. A practical, easy-to-read, and important guide for anyone in higher education."
—**JO BOALER**, Professor of Mathematics Education, Stanford University, best-selling author of *Mathematical Mindsets*, and co-founder of YouCubed.org

"What a fantastic book! As someone who has taught in K–12 and college class-rooms, I have often lamented the fact that K–12 teachers get so much prepa-ration in the skills of teaching, while those at the college level get none. In *Teaching College*, Norman Eng closes that gap brilliantly, synthesizing educa-tion and marketing into a fresh approach that will significantly change the way college classes are taught worldwide. You will find useful insights and practical, actionable tips on every page, and all of it written in an approachable, conver-sational style. A must for anyone who teaches at the college level."
—**JENNIFER GONZALEZ**, Editor-in-Chief at *Cult of Pedagogy*

"I've been in education for almost twenty-five years and in that time I've read a lot of good books about how to improve my teaching practices. *Teaching College* by Norman Eng is hands down the best book I've come across. I'm a faculty developer at a technical college and I lead our New Faculty Develop-ment Program. Over the last year, I've made *Teaching College* our program text. About half of the new instructors I work with have no teaching experience and some of them come in with PhDs in education. Across the board, they have all had positive things to say about the book because Dr. Eng has an uncanny abil-ity to bring clarity to practical and innovative ways to get our students engaged in content."
—**JOEL RANEY**, Asst. Director of Curriculum & Professional Development, Chip-pewa Valley Technical College

Praise for *Create an Engaging Syllabus*

"In this work, Norman zeroes in on the pedestrian task of preparing a syllabus. Many instructors probably consider this endeavor as a straightforward deliv-ery of information. I received many such documents as a student. They were comprised of a couple of typed pages with headings and bullet points. These drab documents never included compelling images or tantalizing hooks. What a missed opportunity! I typically scanned the syllabus and promptly forgot or lost it. Please remember, this is often a student's first interaction with a profes-sor. Wouldn't it be worthy to alter your syllabus so it grabs students and draws them in? Wouldn't it be better to build student engagement and excitement prior to the delivery of the first lesson? If your answer is yes, you picked up the right book!"
—**JAMES STURTEVANT**, author and podcaster, *Hacking Engagement*, and high school Social Studies teacher

"The most powerful section in [Norman Eng's] book, in my experience, was where [he] did side-by-side comparisons of class expectations. My original syllabus was always the left column: negative, punitive, harsh. I believe my new syllabus is more like the right column now . . . Thank you for sharing your insights about syllabi with me. I've gone from handing out a dry packet on Day 1 and not discussing it at all to handing out a colorful and motivating syllabus and taking the time to walk through it with students. It is time well spent."
—**PAMELA MORK**, Associate Professor, Chemistry, Concordia College

"This book totally changed my concept of the syllabus, even though I have taught more than thirty years. Its essential idea is to 'remove 30 percent of your old syllabus' and make it enticing, meaningful, and communicable to your students. It is very easy to read. You can complete reading in thirty minutes and get a life-changing idea."
—**SEOKHEE CHO, PH.D.**, Professor & Director, Center for Creativity and Gifted Education, St. John's Univeristy

PRESENTING.

The Professor's Guide to Powerful Communication

EDUCATIONxDESIGN, Inc.
2585 Broadway #258
New York, NY 10025
norman@educationxdesign.com
Visit the author's website at: https://NormanEng.org

Cover Design by Nina Kim
NinaKimDesign.com

ISBN-13:
eBook: 978-0-9985875-3-0
Paperback: 978-0-9985875-4-7

IF YOU'RE PRESENTING, YOU'RE TEACHING.

FREE VIDEO TRAINING

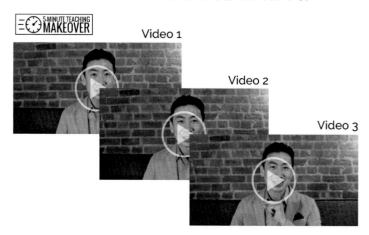

Get the insights that transform your teaching, including how to approach your lectures as well as my 5 recommendations that will captivate your students and 10X their learning.

In this FREE 3-part series, you'll learn:
- My #1 go-to lecture format that captivates students so they're siting on the edge of their seats.
- The 2 biggest myths professors believe about teaching that cause students to disengage (and how to avoid them)
- 5 recommendations to skyrocket student engagement starting with your next lecture.

Access your FREE training here: NormanEng.org/5mtm

TABLE OF CONTENTS

For the students I teach (and taught), the colleagues I work with, and peers around the globe who continue to challenge my worldview and push me to think beyond conventional teaching and presenting.

For my editor, Spencer Borup of Nerdy Wordsmith, who—through his work—reminds me that every single word, sentence, and paragraph matter to powerful communication.

For my parents, Mrs. Margot Eng and Dr. Maximo Eng, who never interrupt or call me during the mornings because they know that's when I write. Their support has been unwavering.

And finally, for my wife, Susana, who does all of the above and more. Thank you, my dear.

PRESENTING.

The Professor's Guide
to Powerful Communication

NORMAN ENG, ED.D

INTRODUCTION

Try this simple test.

Take one of your existing slide decks. Go through it, slide by slide. As you do so, ask yourself, *Do these slides basically duplicate what you're saying?* In other words, do your slides act as a point-by-point outline of your speech?

If so, you've failed the Redundancy Test. Even worse, however—you've failed as a presenter.

Why? Because you as the presenter are no longer needed. Audiences don't need you to read the bullet points. The slides become the main attraction, and you become redundant; at this point, you might as well email them the slides and stay home.

The most offensive question an audience member can ask is, "Will we have a copy of the presentation?" It means we've trained them as students to expect the most important stuff to be in the slides . . . instead of what's coming from your mouth.

It is paramount that we change this mentality—about slides, and about learning.

The fact is, most slide decks are merely outlines. Lecture slides in particular mirror textbooks by going over major points. These three following slides are typical:

THE ROLE OF CULTURE AND SOCIALIZATION

- **Culture**: Patterns of acquired behavior and attitudes transmitted among members of a society (e.g., traditions, beliefs, values)
- **Socialization**: Process of preparing children to function in a group and transmit culture
- **Family** and **school**: Two major institutions that prepare children to function in society

FAMILY

- Family is first medium for transmitting culture
- More than 20% of children live in poverty (African American & Latino children: ~30%)
- Increase in **single-parent** families: One-third of all households with children under 18

OTHER FAMILY FACTORS AFFECTING LEARNING

- Working mothers
- Cohabitation (not married)
- Latchkey children (unsupervised children at home after school)
- Hurried children (deprived of childhood)
- Overparented children (pressure to excel)
- Overindulged (too much material goods)
- Abused / neglected / homeless

Most presenters follow the conventional format: using titles or headers, followed by bullet points

They fail the Redundancy Test, as they only go as far as reflecting what the instructor says. Why then, should students bother reading the textbook? After all, they're getting your CliffsNotes! By designing slides this way, we undermine students' motivation to read—not to mention their interest. No wonder half of audience members surveyed in a Harris Poll admit to doing something else other than focus on presentations.[1]

So what's the alternative?

The short answer is to stop doing what we've always done with slide presentations. Instead, we need to *transform the way we think of and approach presentations*. Presenting has never been about conveying information; presenting is about connecting with the audience.

Communicating.

This book—*PRESENTING. The Professor's Guide to Powerful Communication*—gives you the blueprint.

But unlike most books on PowerPoint,[2] *PRESENTING.* focuses on *them*—the audience. Not on you or your slides. In some cases, you shouldn't even use slides. Regardless, the focus of this book is always on communication, rather than just on presentation.

I won't repeat common advice such as the following:

> *Use more visuals!*
> *Make eye contact!*
> *Show passion!*
> *Practice more!*

Not to mention the dreaded suggestion:

Just have fun!

All of these are vague and unactionable. My goal instead is to elevate your communication effectiveness as a professor and/or presenter through step-by-step recommendations.

In some places, I will show you exact examples of what simple and clear slides look like created by someone *without* a design background. In other spots, I'll show you what expert designers can do. You'll get not only the BEFORE-and-AFTERs, tricks of the trade, and where to go to find great visuals, but also how to approach and plan your presentation *before ever touching your PowerPoint.* No amount of glam can cover up an unclear or hard-to-understand message.

But what if you simply have to cover tons of information? For such instance, I also provide five concrete recommendations that improve the audience experience in the Frequently Asked Questions (FAQ) chapter toward the end.

This book isn't long. You won't find much theory or exposition (even though my recommendations are research- and experience-based). Instead, you get the 80/20—the few things (the 20 percent) that account for the biggest outcomes (the 80 percent). We're all busy, and I want you to read this in one sitting.

Maybe you're wondering, *What's the difference between the countless presentation books out there and one aimed specifically at professors? Why this book?*

For one, professors' presentations aren't always like business presentations. We use theory, research, and lots of data. And, more obviously, we often use slides for the purposes of teaching and learning in the classroom.

Sometimes professors must present at conferences or department meetings as well. So our presentations are less about persuading and pitching, which is what we tend to think of in business.

PRESENTING. shows you how to structure and communicate your content in ways that defy the norm in academia.

Yet *PRESENTING.* doesn't only have to be for professors; anyone who communicates for a living—sales trainers, CEOs, small business owners—can utilize the blueprint from this book as well to connect with their target audience.

I chose to title the book *PRESENTING.* (with a period, or, for my readers abroad, full stop), rather than *PRESENTATIONS,* because the verb captures the appropriate spirit:

Action.

The latter, *PRESENTATIONS,* sounds rather passive. Why? Maybe it's because audiences are so used to feeling bored when they hear the word "presentation."

"Presenting," on the other hand, has a double meaning; it can also be defined as the act of introducing someone or something (as in, "Presenting . . . our new ad campaign!"). This rather elegantly sums up what we do as presenters. We're introducing something *new*. People don't pay attention to something they already know or can guess at. As you'll read about in Chapter 3, novelty triggers attention.

Here's what you can expect to learn in these six power-packed chapters:

Chapter 1. YOUR MINDSET. What is the goal when you present? It shouldn't be to convey information. Rather, slides are designed to do *one* thing. Knowing this goal will forever change the way you think of and prepare slides. A short but powerful chapter that sets the stage for planning.

Chapter 2. YOUR MESSAGE. This chapter helps you gain focus and clarity with a *one-sentence takeaway* template. With it, you won't feel the need to "cover everything"—a deadly mentality that leads to widespread disengagement. Most people walk away from presentations remembering one or two things (and that's with a *good* presentation); nobody remembers five or more. So why do we insist on talking about twenty things? This template will change everything.

Chapter 3. YOUR OUTLINE. Yes, I give you a blueprint for the beginning, middle, and end. But it's much more than that. More importantly is *how* you begin. And it goes beyond an "opening hook." Here's a hint: *Never use important terms and vocabulary up front.* I show you the step-by-step, including examples of topics and slides. After reading this chapter, you'll never start your research presentation with the "conceptual framework" or the "research hypothesis" ever again, nor a lecture with "Today we're going to learn about the theory of Adam Smith . . ."

Chapter 4. YOUR INTERACTIONS. Most presenters leave the audience interaction—typically a Q&A—for the end. Big mistake. The idea is to transform presentations from one-sided affairs into a give-and-take. (Yes, this is what you want even if you're being paid thousands to spread your expertise.) I'll show you the best ways to get audiences involved. Not just the typical four or five people. *Everyone.*

Chapter 5. YOUR DESIGN. In this chapter, we go back to what real design is meant to do: *solve problems*. Not make slides look nice. As such, design will consider the whole experience of the audience *beyond* slides. Besides, most presenters unintentionally design slides that make it hard for audiences to "get." In this chapter, I bring in an instructional designer to streamline unwieldy messes like this:

Chapter 6. FREQUENTLY ASKED QUESTIONS. "What do you do when you have too much to cover?" "What are the best fonts to use?" "Where do we get high-quality visuals?" I'll cover these popular questions and more.

BONUS. CHAPTER-BY-CHAPTER SUMMARY. Looking for the book highlights all in one place? Keep this chapter handy. Not only is there a short paragraph summary for each chapter, this bonus section distills my top insights, "Pro Tips," and quotes from the book that have transformed presentations across thousands of classrooms, conferences, and meetings.

Note that each chapter starts with one key insight. I absolutely hate when the big takeaway is revealed at the end or buried in the text, which forces your students to hunt. To make it easier, I also summarize these insights at the end of each chapter (referred to as "The Bottom Line") and support them with highlighted quotes, "Pro Tips," and videos throughout—all of which are captured in one easy-to-reference Bonus section at the end of the book.

FINAL NOTES.

Most of the PowerPoint slides in this book were created by the author—me. I am not a designer, either self-taught or professional. Anyone with basic knowledge of slideware programs can do this with just a little fortitude. While I do offer insights (and examples) from an instructional designer in Chapter 5, most of my recommendations are based on years of trial-and-error in two industries (marketing and education) and on the latest research in communication, education, media and marketing, and neuroscience. I conduct workshops and teach online courses to professors who want to engage audiences. These are based on my book, *Teaching College: The Ultimate Guide to Lecturing, Presenting, and Engaging Students,* which has regularly topped the Amazon bestseller list in several education categories.

While I cover some mechanics of PowerPoint (e.g., how to highlight certain parts of a data table, how to use the eyedropper tool), this book *does not* show you how to actually use PowerPoint. I won't go over issues like how to create animations or transitions, for instance. For that, I recommend going to the Microsoft Office support site: https://support.office.com/en-us/powerpoint.

This book helps you deal with far more fundamental challenges, such as:

How do I *move* my audience? Engage with them?

What are the components of an effective presentation?
How do I outline it?
What should I include and *not* include?
How do I build instant credibility?
Do I have to follow PowerPoint convention?
How do I "knock it out of the park"?

If you're a professor looking to dramatically transform the way you engage audiences in a short amount of time, *PRESENTING.* is for you. Presenters of any kind who deliver tons of data and content, such as trainers, will also benefit.

Who is this book *not* for? It's not for those who prefer the "old-school" way of presenting. You know, the ones who stand behind the podium and dutifully present the bullet points as laid out on the screen. If that's you, there are plenty of books out there that go into the mechanics of PowerPoint.

PRESENTING. is also not for professors who say they have little time to design slides. Although my system is easy to absorb, it takes time to perfect. And *time* is always a function of *priority*. If you want audiences to leave the room transformed, then you will make it a priority.

Finally, you'll notice I interchange the word "students" with the word "audiences" throughout the book. This is because, as I'm sure you can guess, professors' audiences tend to be made up of students. However, I also include audience members who are conference attendees or colleagues. As you read, just apply the term I use to your particular audience, and you'll be fine.

Ready to turn up your presentation?

Let's start with your mindset in Chapter 1.

[1]This includes sending text messages (28%), emails (27%), and falling asleep (17%). See Nakano (2016): https://blog.prezi.com/presentation-habits-presenters-dont-like-to-admit/

[2]From here on, I use the terms PowerPoint and slide presentations interchangeably. The former has become synonymous with the latter. I'm simply referring to any slideware one might use, including popular tools like Keynote (Apple's slideware application), Google Slides, and Prezi.

01

YOUR MINDSET

KEY INSIGHT:

THINK OF POWERPOINT AS DOCUMENTARIES

I'll bet you never thought of slides this way. But let's take a step back and start with your one goal as presenter: *to make sure the audience gets your message in the shortest time possible.*

Let's start with the first part—*to make sure audiences get your message.* Here, professors often fail right off the bat. They think the goal is singularly to *convey information,* whether they're in the classroom, department meetings, or at conferences.

> **Your goal is to make sure audiences get your message in the shortest time possible.**

The problem is that audiences can and will forget everything you say.

One study found that psychology students who took an intro class ended up knowing only *8 percent more than students who never took the course.*[3] Another study found that anatomy and biochemistry students who earned high grades knew no more than students who received a lower grade—after a short period of time.[4] Or this longitudinal study that found most knowledge gained from a marketing course is lost within two years.[5]

That's depressing. And yet, I'm betting none of this surprises you.

People hear (and see) thousands of messages a day. Their brain can't handle all that info. It's cognitive overload. After all, processing information burns a lot of calories.[6] And to preserve itself, the brain tries to save energy whenever possible.

One way it does this is to shut down. So when students see something like this . . .

---

3 Types of POM Decisions

1. **Production Planning**: Initial stage where managers decide where, when, and how production will occur. Also determine site location and obtain necessary resources.
2. **Production Control**: Decision-making process focusing on controlling quality and costs, scheduling, & day-to-day operations
3. **Improving Production and Operations**: Final stage that focuses on developing more efficient methods of producing goods and services

---

their brains go, *There's too much information in this slide, so I'm just going to shut down. To save energy.*

This is why students check their phones during class.

And really, are we, as professors, any different? All those conference presentations we see can be just as draining. Audiences tune out the details—like the "research methodology" and "conceptual framework"—because they just want the major takeaway so they can be on their way. It's easy to see why most presenters fail in their goal to make sure audiences simply *get the message*.

The second part of your goal as presenter is to get to your point quickly—before their brain shuts down.

In my child development class, students know the point of the class on the first day.[7] I tell them, "Your goal in this course is to answer the question: *How do you develop children into successful adults?*"

And every class I remind them.

Again . . . and again . . . and again.

Until they get tired of it.

It's no different with PowerPoint. That's where this chapter's key insight comes in: **Think of PowerPoints as documentaries.**

With documentaries, a narrator talks over the visuals. You are the narrator. You present (narrate), and slides enhance what you say (visuals).

The key word is *enhance*. Slides aren't supposed to stand on their own. (Remember the Redundancy Test? Go back to the introduction.) They're designed to make your point obvious. Audiences aren't reading on-screen text while watching documentaries! What you hear and what you see is seamless.

▶ STOP AND WATCH

Watch the preview of Ken Burn's documentary, *The Civil War* (1:03). See how the narration and visuals integrate into a seamless learning experience? View at: **https://youtu.be/ IztrtVmthfM**

That's why presentation experts advise using more visuals and less words. Our brains process pictures faster than text—in fact, one study found it's as fast as thirteen milliseconds.[8] The Picture Superiority Effect in full effect, so to speak. With visuals, we don't have to read the slide and listen to the speaker at the same time.

Many presentation experts compare slides to billboards. Billboards, after all, use short, catchy headlines and visuals to attract people's attention. A billboard has mere seconds to communicate its message. Given our parsimonious tendencies, shouldn't slides do the same?

A Coca-Cola billboard with a simple phrase: Taste the feeling.

Yet I prefer comparing slides to documentaries than to billboards. The latter is intended to stand on their own. They don't require narrators. In that way, billboards don't mirror the experience of presenting.

Documentaries, on the other hand, do—and so much more.

Unlike billboards, documentaries use a variety of media, such as videos and music. This can help you think outside the box. Should *you* use videos? Music? Or maybe consider not using PowerPoint at all? After all, some of the best presenters simply talk.

 ## STOP AND WATCH

Watch Sir Ken Robinson's "Do Schools Kill Creativity?" TED Talks speech without slides, which has been viewed over 53,000,000 times—one of the most popular talks of all times. View at: **https://youtu.be/ iG9CE55wbtY**

PRESENTING. When Should You Use (or Not Use) Slides?

Speaking of which, let's tackle this question. The answer is simple: *Use slides only when they help get your point across more quickly. Otherwise, you're better off just talking.*

Remember your goal as presenter? *To make sure the audience gets your message in the shortest time possible* (see Chapter 1).

Use slides only when they help get your point across more quickly. Otherwise, you're better off just talking.

If you think your slides will help you accomplish this goal, then use them. Most presenters, however, don't approach slides that way. They don't think about how to *blend* what they say with what they show on the screen—as documentarians do. Instead, most professors unintentionally duplicate the message, by stating their point out loud *and* showing that same point on the slide.

The result? Both messages compete for the audience's attention and ends up slowing understanding. That's Richard Mayer's Redundancy Principle in effect: People learn better from just graphics and narration than from graphics, narration, *and* on-screen text.[9]

Since most people use slides wrong, experts often suggest minimizing (or avoiding altogether) the use of slides. This way, the audience has no choice but to focus on you.

People learn better from just graphics and narration than from graphics, narration, and on-screen text.

Unfortunately, such advice is misplaced. Just because one doesn't know how to properly season a dish doesn't mean he or she should simply avoid using salt—especially when it makes the dish that much more appetizing.

The solution isn't to advise people to avoid slides. It's far better to show them how to use it. When done correctly, visuals can add weight to your presentation. That's the bottom line.

But aren't there some occasions where it's better off not using slides? Sure.

First, slides don't generally allow for analysis or scrutiny, so if you have a lot of information to convey, consider other ways. Let's say you're teaching faculty members how to navigate a new learning management system (LMS) like Blackboard or Canvas,[10] and you need to show the steps to setting it up. That's information users will likely refer to over and over again.

Wouldn't a handout be more effective? This way, audiences can analyze the details on their own. They're going to request for a copy of your slides anyway (which indicates that there are better ways to communicate your information).

Another alternative is to simply show users how to use the LMS. As the presenter, you might say, "OK, I'm going to walk you through *exactly* how to set up Canvas. You may follow along if you have a laptop or tablet. First, let's look at your navigation bar on the left-hand side of the page. Click on the top link first . . ."

No PowerPoint needed. (If you're really thinking about your audience, then provide both a handout *and* a "how-to" video link as reference. You might decide to go over the finer points from the handout right then and there, which allows audience members to follow along and take notes. They can also refer back to it later. Same with the video.[11])

I'll show you some ways to tackle this issue in Chapter 6, Frequently Asked Questions.

Another situation where you might want to avoid using slides is if you're making a speech. One that is emotionally charged (think Martin Luther King Jr.'s "I have a dream" speech) or aimed to project leadership should focus only on you. Part of the reason is that people tend to equate PowerPoints with conveying information—for better or for worse. So, know your audience.

PRESENTING. THE BOTTOM LINE

Your presentation goal (and approach) is to communicate your message in the shortest possible time by thinking of PowerPoints as documentaries.

In the next chapter, we will focus on your presentation.

[3]Meyers & Jones (1993)

[4]Miller (1962)

[5]Bacon & Stewart (2006)

[6]Swaminathan (2008)

[7]Students often don't know why they're taking a class. Professors know, sure, but do they clearly communicate the purpose, the goal? If it's stated only in the syllabus, under the course description or course objectives section, I bet your students don't read it. To change that, read my ebook, *Create an Engaging Syllabus*, available in major online bookstores.

[8]Potter, Wyble, Hagmann, & McCourt (2014)

[9]Mayer (2009)

[10]Blackboard and Canvas are two popular electronic software applications for delivering educational content, particularly for online courses.

[11]For those who need to show audiences how to navigate a site or use software, most PCs and Macs have built-in software tools to record your voice, the screen, and/or yourself. I also like tools that record and automatically provide a link, like Loom (https://www.loom.com). This frees you from having to upload your recording to a separate site like YouTube or Vimeo. I hit the record button, edit where necessary, and then send viewers the link.

02

YOUR
MESSAGE

CREATE A "ONE-SENTENCE TAKEAWAY"

So, what's your main message? Whatever it is, capture it in one sentence. This is the best way, by far, to dramatically improve your PowerPoint and your presentation as a whole.

But a bit of caution here: do not boil your message down to sentences such as . . .

> *Students will learn about the U.S. banking system.*
>
> *Students will learn about global inequality.*
>
> *Students will learn about color theory.*

These are topics. And topics, by definition, are broad. The minute you teach whole *topics*, you are covering too much in one class or one conference session. Cognitive overload, right? Students won't remember anything you cover. I always imagine reporters standing outside my classroom, asking exiting students, "So what did you learn today?" Kind of like journalists waiting eagerly for a lawyer's soundbite, like you see in those courtroom dramas.

If the student's response is, "I learned about the U.S. banking system," I've failed as a communicator. That's the topic I covered, but it's not learning. Effective lectures and presentations are not about "covering." They're about *un*covering.

> # Teaching is not about "covering"; it's about *un*covering.

You want to *un*cover the most important thing about that topic—the part that students and audiences *need* to know. The one message you want students to be able to articulate to waiting reporters, if you will. Textbooks are responsible for "covering" the rest. When you internalize this, you will enhance audience understanding and engagement.

Let's take our "bad" one-sentence messages from above and focus them:

Students will learn how banks make money off your deposits.

Students will learn that systems affect global inequality more than people.

Students will learn that colors can affect moods and feelings.

See how I took *one* aspect of the topic to deep-dive into?

Here it is spelled out in terms of *topic* and *message*:

Topic	Main Message Students will learn...
U.S. banking system	. . . how banks make money off your deposits.
Global inequality	. . . that systems affect global inequality more than people.
Color theory	. . . that colors affect feeling.

Think about this! In the last example, the takeaway message—i.e., the one thing you want students to internalize—is the power of color. How it affects people. That using different colors sets moods. Evokes feelings. The point is for these students to eventually create effective designs, no?

So, during this presentation, the emphasis isn't on vocabulary terms like *hue, chroma, value*, and *saturation*—even though they're important. The focus is on what they all *mean*. Ultimately, presentations are about the bottom-line message, not the technical stuff along the way.

Look at our banking topic. The focus isn't on covering terms like *expansionary monetary policy* or *macroprudential policy*. It's on helping students "uncover" a system that influences our everyday lives.

The terms merely support your message. Don't let your main message get lost in the terms.

Presenting is like writing a persuasive essay. You always start by connecting with the audience. Never with the technical terms, vocabulary, or details—i.e., the supports. And you always circle back to the main point(s).

But isn't it funny how professors sometimes start with, "OK, today we'll discuss the main theories behind money and banking in the U.S."?

That's a chapter!

What's the main message—the takeaway? What's the one thing you want students to delve into and understand by the end of class? The "post-trial soundbite," so to speak. One message might be, *how banks make money off your deposits.* Another message might be, *how central banks conduct monetary policy to stabilize prices and manage economic fluctuations.*

These are choices you make as presenter. But make a choice.

Same with conference presentations. The point isn't to go over that research project you've been working on—the one regarding a new education approach to help bilingual students. It's not about your research (e.g., articulating your framework, hypothesis, methodology, findings, etc.). The takeaway is the *finding* and *what it means*! That's what audiences come to hear. So, your presentation should emphasize these things during the beginning, middle, and end. (We'll talk more about the structure of your presentation in Chapter 3, Your Outline.)

A Bad Message:
Audiences will learn a new research approach to help bilingual students better improve language acquisition.

A Focused Message:
Audiences will learn that an "experiential learning" approach can help bilingual students acquire language

more effectively by immersing them in more familiar and real situations.[12] (Isn't this what audiences care about? Isn't this what matters? Isn't this an intriguing message?)

So, how do we craft an effective one-sentence message or takeaway?

PRESENTING. The Topic vs. the Message.

First, let's be clear about the difference between a *topic* and *what you teach/present*. Topics are typically the names of textbook chapters, such as:

> Media and Technology
> Chemical Bonding
> Global Inequality
> Money and the Banking System
> Tailoring Techniques for Trousers

Topics could also be the title of your handouts. In a conference setting, your topic may relate to new research, technology, processes, paradigms, or ways of doing something.

Your message, on the other hand, isn't *global inequality* or *tailoring techniques for trousers*. It is a narrow subset of the topic. One way to find your message is to ask yourself, *What do I want my audience to know most about this topic?*

The following criteria can help. What part(s) of your topic is:
1) complex and/or easily misunderstood?
2) a major pillar or principle in your field?

In economics, *supply-and-demand* would qualify (at least compared to, say, the *theory of optimal taxation*). It's complex. It's also a major principle in economics. So take out *theory of optimal taxation* from your presentation or lecture. Here are a few more examples:

Topic	Keep	Potentionally Remove
Postmodern Art	An attitude of skepticism, irony, and rejection of modernist ideas and Enlightenment rationality (using examples from abstract expressionism, performance art, minimalism and pop art)	Institutional critique, Fluxus, and other less well-known postmodern ideas
Sewing techniques	Threading the machine Piping Darts	Princess seams Sewing fur
Statement of financial position (balance sheet)	Assets, liabilities, and equities	Statement of retained earnings

Yes, your presentation is about the most important part(s) of the topic. It's not about covering everything. That's where professors and presenters invariably fail.

The textbook is responsible for covering everything. You, as the presenter, are responsible for magnifying the most important parts.

This is no different when presenting at a conference. While attendees may come in without having read anything about your topic, you still need to distill your research. A great presenter will highlight the part that matters to their audience.

In that way, the worst thing to do is go over the context of your research (i.e., background/framework), your data-collection methodology, your findings, and the implications of those findings—in that order. That's how most of us present research.

The textbook is responsible for covering everything. *You* are responsible for magnifying the most important parts.

PRESENTING. Your One-Sentence Takeaway.

None of it moves people. Even if it's the norm.
Here's your template to create your *one-sentence takeaway*:

> **By the end of the presentation, audiences will be able to [know or do XYZ], so that [their lives will be improved in XYZ way].**

Modify the sentence to fit your situation. Here's an example for a classroom lecture:

> *By the end of the lesson, students will be able to explain how "systems" perpetuate global inequality, so that they can recognize problematic systems and potentially create better ones.*

Here's an example for a conference:

> *By the end of the session, audiences will learn that an*

"experiential learning" approach immerses bilingual students in more familiar and real situations, so that they can acquire language more effectively.

There are two parts of the one-sentence takeaway: the *What* and the *Why*. Define both.

- *What* do audiences need to know (or be able to do) by the end of the presentation?
- *Why* do they need to know (or do) this?

Undoubtedly, the content (the *What*) is important to define. But before you present, you have to be clear about the purpose (the *Why*). In fact, the *Why* is the most important part of your one-sentence takeaway. Without it, people won't care about your presentation. How does your content relate to their lives?

The *Why* drives behavior, according to leadership guru Simon Sinek. In his book, *Start with Why: How Great Leaders Inspire Everyone to Take Action*,[13] Sinek argues that successful organizations understand that people won't buy into whatever is being sold unless they understand *why* they're doing it. Former Apple CEO Steve Jobs, for instance, didn't just market computers (i.e., the *What*); he marketed the idea to challenge the status quo—to "think different" (i.e., the *Why*).

When you present, you're trying to get others to accept your point of view. In the end, you want people to change or act in some way. And audiences won't do that unless they understand *why* the content matters.

Sometimes, the *Why* sounds rhetorical.

Why should students learn how to write a persuasive essay?

Why should they learn about supply-and-demand?

But it's not always obvious to them. Students often think of your lessons in narrow, short-term ways, which is far removed from reality. So I make sure to spell out the *Why* explicitly in every presentation or lesson. I don't assume they know.

PRO TIP!

With classroom presentations, add a *How* to your one-sentence takeaway. This answers the question: *How will your students learn the content?* This is the method, strategy, activity, or tool you want students to use.

For instance: *Students will be able to evaluate the credibility of online sources* (the *What*) **by using the "triangulation" method** (the *How*), *so that they make better buying decisions* (the *Why*).

The *How* specifies the actual learning that takes place.

Here, the one-sentence takeaway evolves into more of a one-sentence *lesson plan*.[14] It crystallizes the three most important parts of your presentation: 1) what students need to know (or do); 2) how they will learn this; and 3) why they ought to learn this.

Chapter 4 will help you flesh out your *How*.

When defining your main message, figure out *Why* people need to hear that message. *That's* what people care about. Without addressing it, you will sound like every other presenter.

---

[12]This topic is used for illustrative purposes only and is not intended to reflect the latest (or actual) studies.

[13]Sinek (2011)

[14]If you want to learn more about how to create a "one-sentence lesson plan," see https://www.facultyfocus.com/articles/teaching-and-learning/focus-your-lectures-with-the-one-sentence-lesson-plan/ (Eng, 2018, September 24)

03

YOUR
OUTLINE

START EVERY PRESENTATION WITH THE *WHY*

"Today, we're going to go over Piaget's theory of cognitive development . . ."

Or maybe:

"In this presentation, I'm going to talk about a new approach to [XYZ] in the mortgage industry . . ."

You ever hear presenters start this way? It's probably the worst way to get attention. Why? Because the brain— the primitive part, at least—tunes out messages that are unclear, complicated, irrelevant, and/or boring. That's 90 percent of messages out there. Which makes sense, since we're exposed to thousands of commercial messages a day.[15] As long as your well-being is not being threatened, your primitive brain[16] will try to ignore the message or spend the least amount of time on it.

Think of your primitive brain as the bouncer at an exclusive club. He's the gatekeeper. He decides if you get in. So, you better stand out in some positive way—whether you're attractive, you've got style, you're a trend-setter, or you have an inside connection. Because in the end, only 10 percent of club-goers get in.

Like the bouncer, your primitive brain is constantly on alert. On the defensive. So it ignores 90 percent of messages directed at you. Only those which are simple, clear, nonthreatening, and novel/intriguing make the cut. Once they do, the midbrain and neocortex can process the message more in depth. Here's where audiences will listen to the content, the details, and the logic.

The bouncer only lets in people who . . .	The primitive brain only lets in messages which are . . .
. . . are attractive	. . . easy to absorb (simple)
. . . have style	. . . clear
. . . set trends	. . . novel or intriguing
. . . have connections	. . . nontheatening/relevant

The bottom line? Ineffective presenters fail because *they communicate with the highly developed part of their brain (reasoning and logic), even though audiences receive the message using their primitive brain (fight-or-flight).*[17]

Ineffective presenters fail because they communicate with the highly developed part of their brain (reasoning and logic), even though audiences receive the message using their primitive brain (fight-or-flight).

And if your presentation is dense, forget it. The brain shuts down.

You need to get to the point fast. Usability design consultant Steven Krug captures that point in the title of his book, *Don't Make Me Think: A Common Sense Approach to Web Usability.*[18] Audiences only care about how your presentation relates to them. In the last chapter, we talked about defining your purpose (i.e., your *Why*). Why is this important to them? So always address the *Why* at the beginning of your presentation.[19]

Let's refer to the "one-sentence takeaway" example for a sociology class (from Chapter 2):

By the end of the lesson, students will be able to explain how "systems" (like the government) perpetuate global inequality, so that they can recognize problematic systems and potentially create better ones.

The *What* and the *Why* are clear:

What you want students to know   *Systems perpetuate global inequality*

Why students should know this   *So they can recognize problematic systems and potentially create better ones*

Now, focus on the last part—the *Why*. How do you relate it to students' lives? How might they **recognize problematic systems and potentially create better ones?**

Certainly not by starting with: "There are three factors that perpetuate global inequality: unfair tax systems, lack of rights among workers, and poor public services."

The better way is to get students to see frustrating systems and structures in their own lives.

So you might start the presentation with a story like this:

"A few weeks ago, I had to buy a new refrigerator for my parents. But right off the bat, the new fridge had problems. It was leaking water. It was all over the inside shelves, which dripped everywhere. A lot of the food went bad. So I had the repair guy come in. He said the door needed readjustment, because it wasn't closing right, and it was letting in warm air. OK, fine. So he fixed the door. But in two days, the fridge was still leaking.

"It took another couple of weeks for the guy to come back, and he said he needed to fix the seal in the door. And guess what? That didn't work either. The guy came five times and couldn't get it right. By then I was like, 'Can't you just authorize an exchange?'

"And the manufacturer kept delaying and delaying. They didn't want to admit their product was bad and issue a credit. They claimed only the store I bought it from can issue credits. But when I talked with the store, they said only the manufacturer can issue approvals in the system, which would then allow the store to exchange the fridge. It's like the right hand wasn't talking to the left hand, and I'm the one that has to deal with the bureaucracy. I'm thinking, *Why can't you guys talk to each other? Why do I have to go back and forth?* I must have spoken with them at least fifteen times over the phone.

"I was *this* close to calling the Better Business Bureau

and one of those news shows where the reporter tracks down rogue businesses and confronts them with a camera crew—you know what I mean? I was ready to give up.

"So, class, let me ask you: Has anything like this—where you're trying to get something done, maybe register for classes, fixing a car, going to the DMV, ordering something and they're rude, whatever—ever happened to you? And you're like, 'I'm never doing business with you guys again'?

"Do me a favor. Think about this for a minute and jot down your thoughts. We'll share your experiences in a bit."

Can you see what I did here? I used a story—a bad experience where I tried to exchange a defective refrigerator—to relate to an otherwise abstract idea: bureaucratic systems. I made the idea concrete. Easy for the audience's croc brains to relate to and accept. I didn't explain how systems perpetuate global inequality first; that's higher-order thinking stuff for later on.

If you start by asking yourself why students should know this idea (the purpose—the *Why*), you can relate it to their lives more easily.

The takeaway: Relating your takeaway message to your audience's lives at the beginning is the single most effective way to 10X your presentation.

Relating your takeaway message to your audience's lives at the beginning is the single most effective way to 10X your presentation.

Let's see how this might work at an education conference, using the one-sentence takeaway from Chapter 2:

By the end of the session, audiences will learn that an "experiential learning" approach immerses bilingual students in more familiar and real situations, so that they can acquire language more effectively.

Again, I've identified the *What* and the *Why*:

What you want the audience to know *An "experiential learning" approach immerses bilingual students in more familiar and real situations*

Why the audience should know this *So bilingual students can acquire language more effectively*

How can I relate this to conference attendees (likely other teachers)? Here's one way:

"By a show of hands, how many of you have bilingual students in your class? OK, great. For me, it's not easy to help bilingual students acquire language. I'm sure many of you know what I mean. Students feel forced to speak about topics that aren't relevant. They hesitate to participate because they don't want to look bad. I get it. So I wanted to do things differently.

"What if we immersed them in *real* situations? Like at a restaurant or a store? Where students have to order food or pay for stuff? That's what I wanted to find out."

This opening would naturally flow into my research on the benefits of the "experiential approach" to instruction. Again, I didn't start with the research. I didn't even start with that term, *experiential approach*. I simply related to the struggles bilingual teachers face.

Now they have context and are ready to hear more.
Now they see a point to being here.
Now they're going to care what I have to say.
Now they're paying attention.

This is how to present effectively. Start with the *Why*.

Unfortunately, professors almost never start their presentations this way. They think more about:

What should I teach?
What goes in this slide?
What examples should I include?

Wrong, wrong, wrong. Those questions should be considered only *after* you've figured out your main message and the reason your message matters. You *start* with the message and the purpose.

Most professors wait until the end to make the "big reveal." Unless you have a good reason to do this, that's almost always a bad idea. Instead, your big revelation up front will sustain the rest of your presentation. Don't make the audience "earn it." Their brains won't wait.

Your big revelation up front will sustain the rest of your presentation. Don't make the audience earn it.

PRESENTING. Your Structure.

Now that you've opened with *Why*, what does the rest of your presentation look like?

First, let's determine your structure. Academic presentation formats are typically related to one of the following:

- Instruction
- Process/Sequence
- Research & Development
- Summary

Instruction. Here the presenter is teaching in the traditional sense, whether lecturing (e.g., the concept of debits and credits) or demonstrating (e.g., how to use a ruler for patternmaking, as one might see in a technical course). Such practice-based or theory-based instruction is usually seen in a classroom or workshop setting.

Process/Sequence. Information is arranged according to a process or a step-by-step sequence. You'll see this in reports ("Here's what we did this quarter . . ."), project roll-outs ("Here's what happened first . . . next . . . last . . ."), or "how-to's" ("The steps needed to get certified in teaching are . . .").

Research & Development. Usually, you'll see these presentations in conferences or graduate courses. Experts reveal their latest findings in their industry. It could be theory-based ("Does mindfulness help us become less sensitive to rejection?") or practice-based ("What evidence-based practices improve patient satisfaction?").

Summary. A summary-type presentation might provide an overview of a topic (e.g., charting the current state of diplomatic efforts in Afghanistan for a political-science class). It might also trace how something has changed over time (e.g., the evolution of teacher education from the normal schools in the late 1800s to the period of scientific efficiency in the early 1900s to the era of competency-based education in the 1960s and '70s).

Note that formats may overlap. For example, a presentation that helps young scholars write more effective grant proposals may be lecture-based (as one might see in a workshop) while also focusing on an itemized process (Step 1, Step 2, etc.).

Since we spent so much time creating one-sentence takeaways (see Chapter 2), you might be wondering: *How does one boil down, for instance, the current state of diplomatic efforts in Afghanistan into one message?*

There's so much to unpack with this particular topic, so I understand why presenters don't even consider simplifying their message. Examples like the above, however, *need* the one-sentence takeaway for that very reason.

Here's where identifying the *Why* helps. Ask yourself, *What is the point of you giving an overview of the current state of diplomatic efforts in Afghanistan?*

Your answer to that question is your one-sentence takeaway.

Presumably, your overview about the current state of diplomatic efforts in Afghanistan leads to some sort of conclusion—whether it is positive or negative. Maybe it's that we need to overhaul our efforts ("Today, I want to show

When you plan your presentation, think about why you're giving audiences all this information.

you why we need a new approach . . .”), or maybe you want the class to problem-solve (“Today, your goal is to evaluate our diplomatic efforts in Afghanistan . . .”)[20]

So when you plan your presentation, think about *why* you're giving audiences all this information.

PRESENTING. Your Outline.

Once you've defined the presentation structure (e.g., instruction, process, research and development, or summary), the next step is to create an outline.

I recommend following a three-step outline called CIA: *Connect, Instruct,* and *Apply.*

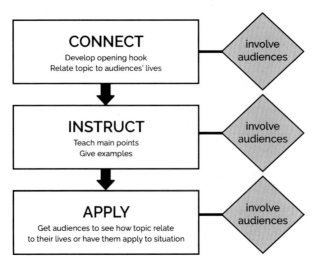

CONNECT
Develop opening hook
Relate topic to audiences' lives

involve
audiences

INSTRUCT
Teach main points
Give examples

involve
audiences

APPLY
Get audiences to see how topic relate
to their lives or have them apply to situation

involve
audiences

Connect. You should *always* open by connecting with the audience. Start with the *Why*, as discussed at the beginning of this chapter. Here's where you determine your "opening hook" as well. It launches your presentation, and the strength of the hook will determine if it's launched into orbit . . . or the ground. Your hook can be any of the following:

- Provocative question
- Anecdote
- Striking statistic or fact
- Analogy
- Scenario/Problem
- Quotation or aphorism

While these hooks are fairly easy to understand, a few notes may help. First, I love opening presentations with a **question.** Audiences feel involved right off the bat. Imagine asking at the start of a sociology lecture, "With a show of hands, how many of you have ever felt the sting of racism?" Think about how this question takes a potentially abstract (and perhaps taboo) topic—*racism*—and immediately makes it relevant.

Also, **stories** are particularly effective at drawing audiences.[21] People often forget facts, but they rarely forget a good story. (Like my anecdote about the defective refrigerator; better yet, do you even remember my alternate opening about the three factors that perpetuate global inequality?) Just remember to connect the story to your topic and to your audience.

A **striking statistic or fact** can also intrigue audiences. "Did you know that 90 percent of an iceberg's volume is below the surface?" Imagine that question leading into a discussion of ice floes in the Arctic—or even an analogy to something else, such as the amount of work that happens behind the scenes of a great film: "Think of the invisible part as the hard work nobody sees . . ."

Scenarios (that pose problems) are another great way to hook audiences. In the classroom, they can encourage problem-solving and critical thinking in the opening minutes. What better way to keep attention? Case studies serve as a perfect example.

PRO TIP!

If you pose a scenario (or anything longer than a sentence), don't post it on the slide *and* read it to the audience. They lose focus as their eyes and ears compete to read and listen at the same time. Do one or the other. Verbalize the scenario out loud (yes, memorize what you're going to say) or post the text on the slide and stay silent as the audience reads it to themselves.

Finally, you can use **quotations** as an opening hook. Imagine putting the following slide on the screen and asking students what this means:

The law is the survival of the fittest . . . The law is not survival of the 'better' or the 'stronger,'. . . It is the survival of those which are constitutionally fittest to thrive under the conditions in which they are placed; and very often that which, humanly speaking, is inferiority, causes the survival.

- Herbert Spencer

In a classroom, I highly recommend asking a *question* or posing a *scenario* as your opening hook. Both require students to get involved immediately. (I'll add *anecdotes* for conference-type presentations.) They draw audiences in even if you're not comfortable with (or unaccustomed to) having audiences participate in the beginning.

Instruct. After you connect with the audience, the content comes next. Any new academic terms or concepts will be anchored to something familiar. For each point or piece of content you present, add examples

> **In a classroom, I highly recommend asking a *question* or posing a *scenario* as your opening hook. Both require students to get involved immediately.**

and always relate back to the *Why*. Also, I strongly recommend involving audiences in your presentation throughout this portion (more on this in Chapter 4).

Apply. The last step is to get audiences to apply the content. In a classroom, this typically means getting students to discuss or work together in some activity. At a research conference, getting audiences to apply what they have learned is similar to what you discuss in the *implications* or *discussion* sections of your presentation: *What does all this mean for me* [the audience]?

Notice how each part of the CIA outline connects back to the audience's perspective. You begin the presentation by connecting with them; as you instruct, you provide relevant examples; and finally, you apply the topic to their world.

That's how you engage.

Relate to the audience at the beginning.

Relate to them in the middle.
Relate to them at the end.

PRESENTING. An Example Outline.

What does a CIA (*Connect, Instruct, Apply*) outline look like for an actual class? Here's an example from my child-development education course.

The topic is *scaffolding*, a term inspired by sociocultural concepts related to Russian psychologist Lev Vygotsky. Basically, *scaffolding* represents a way teachers can help children learn, by providing guidance—or "temporary supports" (much like a scaffolding props up a building)—until it is no longer needed.

Using an essay template is a scaffolding strategy. Children need it in the beginning, as reference, but eventually, templates won't be necessary. Another example of scaffolding is *chunking*. Breaking up a long text into shorter "chunks" helps students comprehend. How about getting students to use "word webs"? It's a great way to organize their thoughts before writing. Ultimately, I want children to be able to write an essay, comprehend a book, or organize their thoughts without these explicit "supports."

Examples of Scaffolding	Explanation
Essay template	Provides students with a structure (intro, conclusion, etc.)
"Chunking"	Helps them comprehend more easily
Word webs	Organizes their thoughts before writing

Here's my one-sentence takeaway for a presentation on the topic of *scaffolding*:

By the end of class, students will be able to apply "scaffolding" techniques to various classroom topics, so that they can teach more effectively and help children become independent learners.

Again, I've identified the *What* and the *Why*:

What you want the students to know *Scaffolding and how to apply it*

Why students should know this *So that they can teach more effectively and help children become independent learners*

Ready for the presentation outline using CIA?

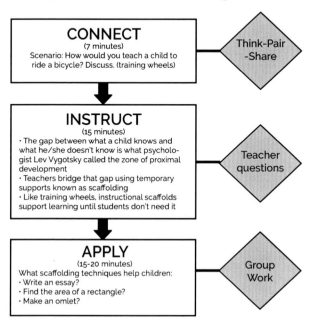

The *Why* informs my opening (Box #1: *Connect*). I want students to teach more effectively, right? What better way to do that than to ask them how to teach a child to ride a bike? This takes one slide at the most—or maybe you don't need a slide at all!

Through a *think-pair-share* exercise, students generate ideas, pair up to discuss, and then share their results with the class.

Now I can move into the content (Box #2: *Instruct*). Students will learn key points about Vygotsky's *zone of proximal development* (ZPD) and how it relates to instructional scaffolding. Defining it and providing examples should only take a few slides at the most.

Finally, we can apply what students learn (Box #3: *Apply*). One slide—that's it!

(Also note the diamond-shaped boxes to the right, which represent opportunities for audience involvement. More on this in Chapter 4.)

All told, this presentation needs five slides at most. Maybe fewer.

Notice below how I use *every opportunity* to relate to students or make things more concrete:

Beginning: "How would you teach a child to ride a bicycle?"

Middle: "Have you ever seen scaffoldings on buildings? How is instructional scaffolding just like training wheels?"

End: "What scaffolding techniques would you use for the following . . . ?"

Here are my slides, side-by-side with the outline:

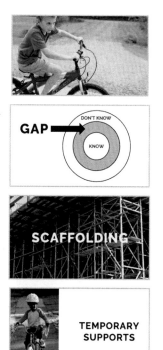

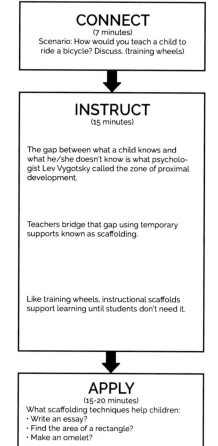

Granted, I simplified this presentation. For example, I could have added a slide about psychologist Lev Vygotsky, who developed the theory related to the *zone of proximal development*, or multiple slides breaking down ZPD. Regardless, heed to the "less-is-more" dictum.

Remember, you're fighting the clock. Students will mentally check out in twenty minutes (or sooner!) unless you liven things up. Get them involved.

You're also fighting nature. The audience's brains will shut down to save calories whenever possible. Like a drunk patron trying to get into a club, your content will be turned away. The only way to make it past students' "primitive" brains—and into their higher functioning neocortex—is to make your presentation novel, simple and focused, and relevant.

See how the previous slides have little to no text? Just the way audience's brains want messages to be. Simple.

If you're struggling to simplify your presentation, just remember: of the twenty things you want to cover today, students won't remember more than a few things, according to experts.[22]

Also, you might have noticed the time limits in the example. My actual instruction—the lecture part—is no more than fifteen minutes. Why? Audience attention tends to drop dramatically beyond that.[23] It's why TED Talk events last about eighteen minutes. It's one unit of optimal attention span. So, anytime you talk about technical content—the abstract concepts, terms, and famous figures—remember to keep it short.

> **Of the twenty things you want to cover today, students won't remember more than a few things.**

If you have a lot to cover, then divide the lecture into fifteen-minute segments. Interact with audiences in between (again, more on interaction in Chapter 4).

Finally, notice the economy of words in each slide. They support your talk—just as visuals do in a documentary. This is a critical mindset discussed in Chapter 1.

Here, the outline is no different. Let's start with what *not* to do:

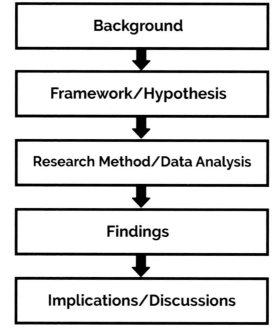

The above outline is for a research paper, not a presentation. Talking point by point about your research— the background, the framework, the research method, etc.—make little sense.

Why?

Because presentations aren't about transmitting information. Presentations are about convincing attendees that your research conclusion is valid and deserves more attention. The goal is to persuade, convince, and influence—and get audiences to act.

Don't you want them to contact you, extend your study, implement your findings, and/or otherwise spread the word? Isn't that the point?

If so, then scrap the research paper format.[24] Instead, focus on *Connect, Instruct, Apply* (CIA), as we did with the "scaffolding" topic.

Let's try it. The topic I brought up earlier was a study on the experiential approach to bilingual education. Here's how CIA is applied to the beginning and end (note the middle "content" part—the details—is beside the point, and therefore have been left blank):

CONNECT
"One of the biggest struggles teaching bilingual students is helping them speak more authentically ... But what if we immersed them in real situations? Like at a store or market? ... So, in our study, we had children immersed in real talk. And guess what we found? [Summarize]

INSTRUCT
(10 minutes)

· Framework
· Hypothesis
· Research method
· Results/Data

APPLY
(5-10 minutes)
Discussion: What does experiential learning actually look like in the classroom?

(Note: ellipses in the boxes indicate areas to elaborate.)

By flipping the script—starting with the findings instead of the background/hypothesis—we pass the gatekeeper in the croc brain, the filter, that asks:

> *Is the message easy to understand?*
> *Is it simple and clear?*
> *Is it novel?*
> *Is it relevant to me?*

Presenting research findings and implications upfront— especially if they are surprising—immediately hooks the audience. Here, the major finding is that the experiential approach has shown some significant increases in language performance.

Same with the implications—the "Why should I care?" part. In this case, it answers the audience's question, *What do the results of this study mean for me?* Do not put this last, as most research presenters do.

To end, the presenter can talk about ways in which to apply this research: *What does experiential learning look like in the classroom?* Once again, we circle back to the audience.

PRESENTING. THE BOTTOM LINE

The *Why*—the purpose—is your new way to open presentations. When planning your outline, the first question you ask is: *Why am I presenting* [Topic XYZ]?

Your answer informs the opening. Find that hook! Once it is established, the content follows. This approach may radically depart from the way you used to present, but your audience will be immediately engaged. You want them to reach that moment of clarity—that *Aha!* moment, as presentation expert Jerry Weissman calls it.[25]

That won't happen when logic is employed at the start. The audience's primitive brains simply won't allow it. Get past that gatekeeper by being novel, simple, clear, and relevant. *Connect, Instruct, then Apply.* CIA.

Next, we build audience involvement.

---

[17]Klaff (2011)

[18]Krug (2005)

[19]Once audiences have "bought into" your message, their brain will allow you to do more in depth to get to the more complex stuff. That's not to suggest you get lazy and just stuff content into the latter part of your presentation. We'll discuss how to present complicated material, such as data, in Chapter 5.

[20]Is PowerPoint even the best way to provide an overview of the diplomatic efforts in Afghanistan? Maybe the better way is to summarize them in a handout. Have students read it before or during class. Wouldn't the subsequent discussion or activity be more fruitful? When I see a "summary" topic—which, again, must by definition cover a lot of information—I question whether it would be better dealt with in a format that allows students to study it more closely, as they would with a handout. Slides aren't always the best option, as I argue in Chapter 1 under the section: "When Should You Use (or Not Use) Slides?"

[21]See Esther Choy's *Let the Story Do the Work: The Art of Storytelling for Business Success* (2017).

[22]See Goodman (2006)

[23]See Goodman (2006); Malmsfors, Garnsworthy, & Grossman (2004); Penner (1984); Stuart & Rutherford (1978)

[24]Note that I'm not suggesting you remove important research information, such as the framework, hypothesis, and data analysis. I'm merely suggesting you "repackage" it in a way that resonates.

[25]Weissman (2009).

04

YOUR
INTERACTION

INSERT AUDIENCE INTERACTION EVERY TEN MINUTES

If you're lecturing for forty-five minutes straight . . . you're doomed.

As described in Chapter 2, the audience's brains are finding any excuse to reject messages and conserve calories. And even if you keep within the recommended twenty-minute limit, students will likely experience frequent lapses in attention, alternating between being engaged and *not* being engaged in ever-shortening cycles throughout the duration of your presentation. In one study, students actually reported lapses *thirty seconds after class began*, followed by more lapses four and a half minutes into the lecture.[26]

This means students aren't paying attention continuously even for fifteen minutes, nor even for *five* minutes—let alone for longer. Fewer lapses occur, however, when teachers use "non-lecture" instruction: demonstrations, group work, questioning, etc.

This chapter shows you how to build audience involvement into presenting.

Most importantly, you want to involve the audience in some way every ten minutes or less. That change-up "restarts the 'attention' clock."[27] If you question students regularly—bravo! You're doing that in some way already.

Most instructors, however, even mess up the questioning. They'll lecture about, say, *race and ethnicity*, pause, and then ask, "OK, can anyone tell me the differences between the two?"

Instructors know what happens next. Only a few students will raise their hands and participate. The majority will stay silent and uninvolved, which is a perennial problem. Part of audience involvement is literally that—involving the entire audience. The standard for effective classroom participation, therefore, isn't to get *some* students to talk. It should be to get *everyone* actively involved.

Questions like the above—posed to the class in this traditional manner—won't force every single member to process what they learn. So, how can you ensure full involvement?

> **The standard for effective classroom participation isn't to get some students to talk. It should be to get everyone actively involved.**

PRESENTING. 3 Ways to Involve Audiences: *Talking*, *Writing*, and *Tapping*.

Talking. One popular technique is "turn-and-talk." In the K–12 world (especially in the younger grade levels), turn-and-talk is widely used.

Say you've just lectured on a particular topic for ten minutes. Instead of merely pausing to ask a question, tell students to turn to a fellow classmate and discuss what you just taught. They could: 1) discuss their responses to the question posed; 2) explore or brainstorm solutions; or 3) summarize what you lectured. Based on which type of *turn-and-talk* you use, your prompt might sound like one of the following:

Discipline	Type of Turn-and-Talk	Prompt
Chemistry	Question-Answer	**"Why is air classified as matter? Do me a favor—turn and talk to someone next to you and discuss."**
American Literature	Exploration	**"What would *Pride and Prejudice* look like if it were written from Mr. Darcy's point of view? Discuss some of your thoughts with a partner."**
Marketing	Brainstorm	**"OK, now I want to hear from you. What are some possible solutions to alleviate 'buyer's remorse'? Turn and discuss with someone at your table."**
Economics	Summary	**"With a partner, can you summarize the difference between *macroeconomics* and *microeconomics*?"**

In each of these cases, students are retrieving information (*out* of the brain), rather than passively absorbing content (*into* the brain) as they might during lectures. *Out* versus *in*.

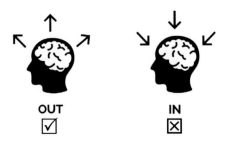

OUT ☑   IN ☒

During this retrieval process, information transfers from short-term working memory to long-term memory.[28] That's where information sticks. Yet, given the way most instructors present, this transfer doesn't happen regularly enough. And part of the reason is because we don't push students to consistently retrieve information. Consistently, as in *several times* during the course of a presentation or lecture. One-sided lectures, where teachers do most of the talking, still prevail in the higher education classroom.[29]

PRO TIP!

Use *turn-and-talk* when students aren't raising their hands. Sometimes I'll ask a question, realize that no one wants to participate, and say, "You know what? Work out the answer with a partner." More hands will go up afterwards, as now students are better prepared.

Retrieval practice doesn't have to take much time. Turn-and-talks should last no more than two minutes. Your job is to walk around the classroom and listen in. That's the accountability mechanism. It ensures students stay on topic and reveals areas of confusion or misconception. In the end, turn-and-talks are about assessing students' knowledge *and* assessing your teaching. You'll know instantly if you haven't been clear.

After two minutes, we'll reconvene: "OK, let's share some of what you talked about." Here's an opportunity to cold-call students and clarify misconceptions.

Turn-and-talk is my go-to move.

Writing. Writing is another way to get everyone involved. It increases rigor by adding intentionality and formality. Furthermore, it pushes students to turn vague notions they might have had while thinking—or even talking—into complete thoughts.

One writing process I use is "stop–jot–share."

Similar to turn-and-talk, you lecture or present your material for a short period of time (around ten minutes). Then, **stop**. Ask students to **jot** down everything they remember (or summarize the material discussed). Finally, have students **share** their responses with a partner and fill in any missing gaps.

Here's stop–jot–share in action:

"OK, class, I just spent the last ten minutes going over the major differences between *impressionism* and *modernism*. Let's stop for a minute. Take this time now to summarize the most important points in a paragraph. I'll give you two minutes."

After students have finished, say, "Now, turn to someone next to you and read what you wrote. When both sides are done, I want you to plug in any gaps in your own notes."

Simply put, stop–jot–share takes turn-and-talk to the next level.[30]

Tapping (and Clicking). So far, I've discussed involving students through talking and through writing. The third idea to prompt whole-class involvement is through technology. Online tools like Quizlet (quizlet.com), Pear Deck (peardeck.com), and Kahoot! (kahoot.com) get students to respond using their digital devices (i.e., smartphones, tablets, or laptops). It's a fun, low-stakes way to assess students' understanding periodically and regularly.

Let's say during my presentation I described the differences between *fact, opinion, belief,* and *assumption.* I want to check in on students and assess their understanding. Using Pear Deck, for instance, I can pose a question on the overhead, such as:

> *"Breakfast is the most important meal of the day."*
> *What kind of statement is this?*

Students see four options on their device and choose one by tapping (on their smartphone or tablet) or clicking (on their laptop). Responses can then be projected, as shown below:

Think of the resulting conversation. Students can defend their choices, build

A: Opinion	6
B: Belief	7
C: Fact	9
D: Assumption	0

off each other's ideas—I can even address misconceptions on the spot (as opposed to waiting for students to make the same mistakes on a midterm exam). Think about how much more they would appreciate this.

Pear Deck, as well as other online assessment tools,[31] offers options for open-ended responses, polls (see below for example), and even drawings, which make interactions more fun.[32]

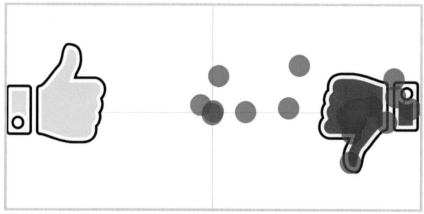

Polling students with a scatterplot, as shown here using Pear Deck, can serve as a starting point for discussion

Other applications—like Padlet (padlet.com) and Flipgrid (flipgrid.com)—give students a chance to create content and share it with the class, rather than just answer quiz-type questions.

For instance, during one of my classes in mathematics methodology (which trains childhood-education majors to teach math), undergraduate students divide circles into equivalent portions freehand. This helps them experience the struggles children face understanding the concept of fractions and equal parts. Students then post their drawings—their best and worst ones—on the Padlet "wall" (see screenshot).

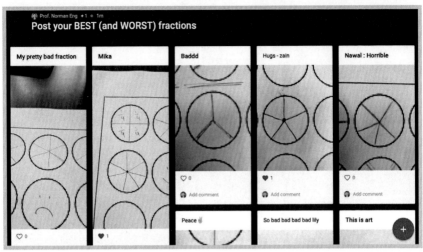

Tools like Padlet, above, get everyone to post their ideas

Imagine the possibilities. Aside from drawings, students could also post written responses, images, videos, and even audio recordings. Talk about full-class participation and engagement!

The key is to involve audiences at very specific times while presenting. That's why the outline template from Chapter 2 included diagonal boxes as part of the planning phase.

Here's a list of ideas to involve your audience (some of which I already discussed), along with descriptions or suggestions on the right. All of them meet the gold standard for involvement: 100 percent audience participation.

Involve Audiences Via...	Example or Further Description
Turn-and-talk prompts	"Turn to someone next to you and discuss . . ."
Stop–jot–share prompts	"Let's pause and take three minutes to write down everything related to . . ."

Involve Audiences Via...	Example or Further Description
Audience poll/survey	Get the audience to raise hands or use digital apps like Poll Everywhere and Pear Deck
Human Spectrogram Live Barometer	Audience members/students "vote with their feet," by walking to various corners of the room to indicate their answer. They then have to defend their choice.
Quizzes	Via paper-and-pencil or online apps like Quizlet
Content creation	Flipgrid, Padlet
Speed-networking Concentric Circle	Much like the concept of speed-dating, members sit (or stand) opposite a partner and discuss questions you pose for two minutes. When it's time for the next question, students rotate to a new partner. With concentric circles, you have an outer circle of students facing an inner circle of students.

PRESENTING. THE BOTTOM LINE

When planning the content part of your presentation, think about involving every single audience member in some way. That's the gold standard for participation. The rules shouldn't change, even for conference presentations. Asking attendees to raise their hands for an informal survey or dividing into small groups to discuss their thoughts about a topic and then sharing with the rest of the audience (much as students would in a turn-and-talk exercise) can liven any presentation. Even if it's focused on research.

[26]See Bunce, Flens, and Neiles (2010)

[27]See Middendorf & Kalish (1996)

[28]For more, see for instance Brown et al. (2014), Cranney et al. (2009), or McDermott et al. (2014)

[29]Research in various fields supports this; see, for instance, Eagan et al. (2014), Stains et al. (2018), and Watts & Schaur (2011).

[30]For details on stop–jot–share, see https://normaneng.org/introducing-stop-jot-share/ (Eng, 2018, April 23)

[31]Popular tools to assess and engage audiences (some of which are mentioned in this chapter) include Poll Everywhere (polleverywhere.com), Mentimeter (mentimeter.com), Flipgrid (flipgrid.com), Kahoot! (kahoot.com), Quizlet (quizlet.com), Padlet (padlet.com), and Pear Deck (peardeck.com).

[32]While free for basic features, these tools may charge for premium features

05

YOUR
DESIGN

CONSIDER THE "USER EXPERIENCE" (UX)

For this book, I almost chose the following cover design:

It's simple, elegant, and bold—as if it sprang from the pages of *Communication Arts* or *IDN Magazine*. Compared with the other options, this cover stood out.

But experience has taught me to always test assumptions, including what I assumed would make an effective book cover. So, I polled my students, my various online communities, professors, and, face-to-face, my friends.

In the end, this cover polarized voters. Critics felt like it was extra work to tilt their head to read the title, even though some agreed it was well designed.

Which, if I'm being honest, absolutely crushed me.

The point here isn't to poll audiences; rather, it's to consider what they think about and go through *as* they listen to your presentation. Are there areas that might confuse them? Turn them off? Require clearer examples?[33]

This is all part of the *user experience* (UX), a critical aspect of effective communication and relationship building. In business and design, *user experience* refers to the overall experience a customer has with a product or service. It might include the process of searching for and finding a book online, or checking out said book, or unboxing the merchandise, or, if necessary, returning it.

The UX asks: Was the experience easy or difficult for the customer?

Think about the frustrating experience I described in Chapter 3 in which I tried to return a defective refrigerator. Scheduling multiple service repairs, talking with customer service for months, and bouncing back and forth between the dealer and manufacturer were all obstacles that added up to a nightmare UX—a user experience that ensures I won't buy their products again.

Every time you present, you create a UX—whether you intend to or not. The questions then become:

Have you created a positive or negative user experience? Have you made it easy or hard for audiences to understand and engage?

Every time you present, you create a user experience —whether you intend to or not.

Often times, professors don't ever consider this.

And they wonder why students zone out.

The way you design presentations shapes audiences' user experience. But it's not about making beautiful slides. You don't have to be a graphic designer. Instead, the goal of design is to help audiences get from point A to point B as quickly as possible. Removing the "friction" in your slides is one way to do this.

Remember: as presenters, we're trying to get past our audiences' first lines of defense— that croc brain that asks one question: *Is it safe to ignore the message?* If the content is

The goal of design is to help audiences get from point A to point B as quickly as possible. Removing the "friction" in your slides is one way to do this.

boring, unnecessarily complex and/or abstract, irrelevant, too long, or too familiar, the brain will shut down. All to conserve calories and save energy.[34]

So, anything that causes "friction" in the mind—a disconnect, a moment of confusion, the need to exert/expel unnecessary energy—will make it harder for audiences to understand your message. And the more friction that exists, the more likely audiences tune out.

What are examples of friction?

> Complicated tables or charts
> Blocks of text or too much information
> Being too abstract
> On-screen text that is hard to see
> Slides that don't flow

Nina Kim, Associate Director at the Center for Digital Education at Washington University, agrees. She helps faculty members communicate lectures and presentations more clearly through design,[35] so I consulted her expertise. Nina boils it down to three things:

> SIMPLIFY.
> COMPOSE.
> CREATE RELATIONSHIPS.

SIMPLIFY.

Let's delve into each.

In theory, most of us know this. But we don't necessarily apply it. Usually, it's because we think one (or more) of the following:

> 1. *College is supposed to be hard (we're all adults here!)*
> 2. *It takes too much time to make content simple and easy to understand*
> 3. *There's just too much material to cover*

This mentality violates what we know about the croc brain. Reducing cognitive load is critical—which means minimizing friction. To help you simplify, Nina recommends remembering two words: *distill* and *distribute*.

Distill and *distribute* (or D&D, as I call it) are the two most effective design principles to instantly simplify and improve the way audiences respond to you. Our first task is to make sure that our content has been distilled to its most concise and clear form. When designing your slides, ask yourself:

> ### *Distill* and *distribute* (D&D) are the two most effective design principles to instantly simplify and improve the way audiences respond to you.

Is anything repeated?
Can I say something with fewer words?
Would a picture make a better example than written text?

Let's take an example of a typical slide one might present on climate change:

Earth's ice is melting fast

- Human activity (burning fossil fuels that lead to greenhouse gases) is major cause
- The snows in Kilimanjaro have melted more than 80% since 1912
- Himalayan glaciers could disappear by 2035
- Arctic sea ice has thinned significantly over past 50 years

While it's not the worst slide out there, it can be improved. Let's walk through the process to distill it.

First, make sure the slide only communicates one idea. Here, the point is that ice is melting fast, so I want to eliminate anything unrelated, such as the human factors (i.e., the first bullet point). That can go in the next slide. I want to keep this slide about that one overarching idea.

Next, eliminate the "fillers." This includes words like *has* or *the*. What are the most important words to keep? Simplified bullet points should look more like a newspaper headline, as seen here:

Earth's ice is melting fast

- Snows in Kilimanjaro: 80% melted since 1912
- Himalayan glaciers will disappear by 2035
- Arctic ice thinned over past 50 years

After you've deleted unnecessary words, think about *distributing*. Can you spread your points across multiple slides? Again, the goal is to have one idea per slide. Let's refer back to the climate change slide.

First, do we need the heading here? We use them in every slide because that's the default format in PowerPoint; from a design standpoint, however, the large type of headings draws the eye, and since it stands out, audiences subconsciously assign more importance to it compared to the body.[36]

While the heading ("Earth's ice is melting fast") is important, it doesn't need to be on every slide. Separate it into its own slide. Subsequent slides that fall under this section don't need reminders.

So, the header is in its own slide, and I've eliminated it from the rest. But we're not done. Next, let's tackle the bullet points. Is it necessary to display all three facts on the screen?

For every bullet point, every sentence, and every word you put up, ask yourself if it can be referenced out loud instead. Often times, it can. When audiences are forced to read on-screen text and listen at the same time, their auditory and visual channels compete to absorb information. And people lose focus. That's the *redundancy principle* mentioned in Chapter 3.

So, let's distribute each bullet point into its own slide, like the following:

By now, you've made tremendous progress—simply by distilling and distributing.

Before

After

With the BEFORE version, too much friction exists. First, too many ideas are being communicated (four bullet points plus one heading). Second, the text is dense. And third, the slide is uninteresting. All three issues guarantee the primitive croc brain will ignore the slide.

But the AFTER group of slides align with the croc brain's desire to conserve energy. It's simple, easy to read, and visually arresting. The message is clear. The friction has been effectively minimized.[37]

PRO TIP!

When using visuals, fill the whole slide with the image. Go borderless. Images then become much more vivid. It sounds obvious, but non-designers often don't think to do that. They subordinate the image to the text, which often leaves it as an afterthought. Think of the visuals used in documentaries.

 RESOURCE ALERT: Looking for high-quality, free visuals? Check out the Q&A at the end of the book for my best recommendations!

By the way, it doesn't matter how many slides you have. Some experts recommend one to two slides per minute, whereas others say ten slides for every twenty minutes.[38] While helpful, I would rather have twenty visually appealing slides that get your point across than five text-heavy slides that leave audiences confused.

Furthermore, this spaced-out version adheres to the "documentary" mindset discussed in Chapter 1: Each slide is highly visual and seamlessly supports the presenter's narration.

That's user experience.

COMPOSE.

After you simplify, consider the *composition*. Where you place things and how big they are in relation to each other has a big influence on how audiences interpret design. Nina believes that the goal with composition is three-fold: *to create interest; to create balance; and to create a visual hierarchy.*

Interest. The key is to vary slide compositions. Audiences grow bored when content is static (remember the croc brain?). Here are Nina's examples of an image with a small amount of text on a slide, including three arrangements that create interest.

PHOTOSYNTHESIS:
The process by which green plants and some other organisms use sunlight to synthesize foods from carbon dioxide and water.

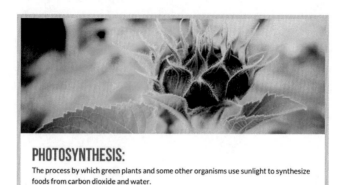

Of course, not every concept will be as breathtaking to visualize as photosynthesis. The point is: *Don't simply drop information into the template the way PowerPoint has it laid out for you.* The next slide illustrates a typical way that novices might present photosynthesis.

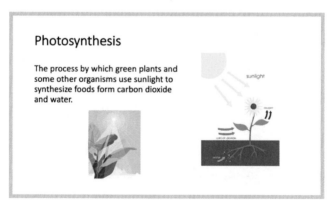

Such presenters fill up empty spaces with multiple pictures. This merely adds noise by cluttering the slide. Unless you have a reason, stick to one visual and make it the "hero shot."[39]

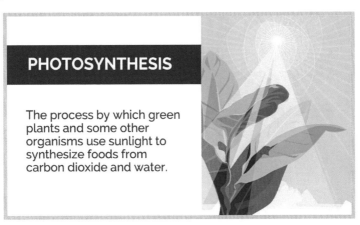

While not as stunning as the first three, it's a vast improvement over the previous. Gone are the multiple images, the inconsistency, and the "drag-and-drop" feel.

PRO TIP!

Use the Eyedropper tool to match colors in your slide. That sense of cohesion reduces the friction and improves the user experience. To learn how to use the Eyedropper tool, search online with the phrase "use Eyedropper to match colors on your slide" or check the support site for Microsoft Office (support.office.com).

CREATE RELATIONSHIPS.

Finally, Nina recommends creating relationships between your design elements by using repetition, alignment, and proximity. Help your viewer make connections *between* your content both on individual slides and between slides. You can use repetitive design elements such as color, size, and composition to train your viewer to associate pieces of information. As an example, let's say that every time a key term appears in your slide deck, it's incorporated into a "callout box" similar to the one below.

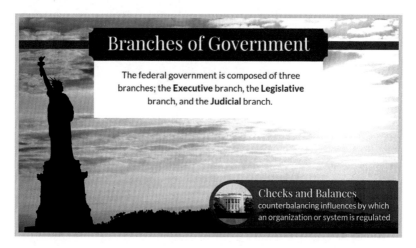

As a viewer, every time I see a red callout box with a bolded word and definition underneath, I can quickly categorize that piece of information because of the ***repetition*** of design elements.

For most of you, the simplest tweak to create repetition is to match the text color with the image color. Take the previous photosynthesis slide: I could make the header and body text green to match the image via the Eyedropper tool (see Pro Tip in previous page).

Alignment is another key to creating relationships. Our brains automatically associate things that are aligned. As you build your slide compositions, take the time to align objects. Nowadays, many slide-creation applications (such as Canva.com) help you align your elements with little grid lines that will indicate whether or not your objects are aligned.

Closely related to alignment is **proximity**. As with alignment, our brains automatically associate objects that are close to each other. In contrast, we disassociate objects that are far away from each other. Use proximity to your advantage, in conjunction with alignment, to indicate that your pieces of content belong with one another.

Balance. This can be achieved through *symmetry* and *asymmetry*. Symmetrically balanced designs, according to Nina, will use objects of the same size placed an equal length away from the center of the slide. Asymmetrically balanced designs will use objects of different sizes (say one large and one small) and offset these objects in order to create balance. Notice how both please the eye in the example below.

Use *symmetry* (left) and *asymmetry* (right) to create balance

Visual hierarchy. Finally, we want to use our compositions to create a visual hierarchy. It is going to tell audiences how they should interpret the importance of your slide's content.

Objects placed toward the top of your composition—for example, a slide heading—will be interpreted as more important. Elements larger in size will also be interpreted the same way. Make sure to use size and placement to your advantage to show your viewer how to interpret your design.

PRO TIP!

Consider removing your slide headings or making them smaller. It's interesting how PowerPoint (and other slideware) default to having a heading in each slide. Its large size suggests it's really important! Yet the body is often more important and therefore it should be upgraded, from a visual hierarchy perspective. Ask yourself, *Is the heading even necessary?*

→ Other Family Factors Affecting Learning

- Working parents
- Cohabitation (not married)
- Latchkey children (unsupervised children at home after school)
- Hurried children (deprived of childhood)
- Overparented children (pressure to excel)
- Overindulged (too much material goods)
- Abused / neglected / homeless

Forget the fact that this slide has too much information. What's more important here, the heading or the bullet points? In most cases, it makes more sense to:
1) remove the heading; 2) make it smaller; or
3) separate it into its own slide.

Do all these changes actually matter?

Maybe these tweaks don't mean much to you. All that time and effort for what? It's the content that matters, right?

When you present in front of industry experts, it's easier to stuff content: their knowledge is more sophisticated compared to that of novices, so presenters can afford to go heavier on information. This may explain why professors teaching advanced biochemistry, for instance, may feel that design and visual flourishes are a waste of time. Graduate level students or conference attendees don't require such visual "crutches."

Yet we're *all* subject to cognitive overload, novice and expert alike. All messages are still received by the primitive fight-or-flight brain. It still pays to be simple, novel, and concrete.

In the end, changing the type size from 28-point to 40-point may not mean much on its own (although the audience member in the back of the room may appreciate it), but combined with other design principles—namely *simplicity*, *composition*, and *relationships*—the collective UX will improve.

It's like being nice to people. Once won't necessarily make a significant impression, but if done consistently, people will generally see you that way. In this way, design matters tremendously.

PRESENTING. How to Show Data.

Sometimes we can't escape highly detailed sets of information, such as data, charts, graphs, and complex diagrams. If you need to show this type of information in your slides, keep in mind the following three recommendations.

Recommendation #1: Only show what is necessary. Instead

of including the whole table, only provide the column headings, along with the rows of information that are most applicable. If you are working with a data or a graph, make sure to eliminate any unnecessary labels. Seriously— often times, you don't even need the numbers!

Recommendation #2: *Simplify where possible.* This goes back to Nina's recommendation to distill information; in this case, data. Do you need to present a graph, or can you sum up with a single percentage? Do you need to present individual points of data, or can you describe trends? Taking the time to do this extra step often eliminates unnecessary information—that *friction* I talked about—and helps your audience home in on the most important statistic.

You can also simplify the data graphics themselves. For instance, with a pie chart, try to consolidate your data so that there are less divisions. The only slice that matters is the one you want to highlight. Don't let the others clutter your message.

If you're showing a scatter graph, consider creating one that shows just the trend line instead of each and every data point.

See the sample graph below:

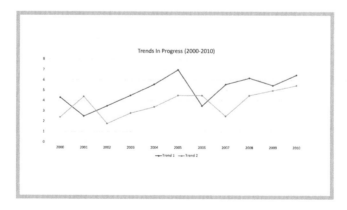

This is the default created in PowerPoint when you click on *line graph*. But there are a few problems: the labels are really small; the lines can be distracting; the title is hard to read; and if the trend is what's important then the points on the lines aren't needed.

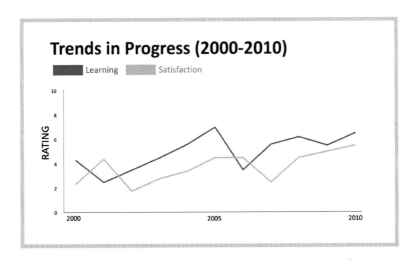

With the new and improved graph, we've minimized the friction by: 1) recreating and enlarging the title, legend, and vertical axis; 2) deleting the background lines; 3) thickening the graph lines; and 4) displaying select numbers for the vertical and horizontal axes.

But wait . . . do I even *need* the slide heading? The dates in parentheses are already indicated on the x-axis. I could just allude to the heading by saying out loud, "The trend over the last ten years indicates that online course satisfaction could be better . . ." Now I don't need the "Rating" label. And if you make one minor tweak, you don't even need the *key*.

With the next slide, we've minimized the "drag" on cognitive load. All that's left is what matters.

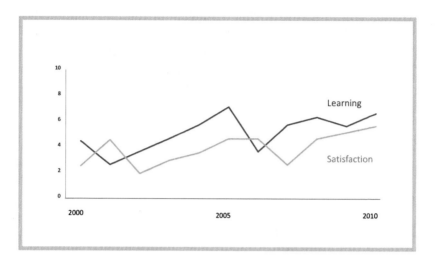

Recommendation #3: *Use strategic highlights.* Don't make viewers work so hard to find which part of the chart you're focusing on. Draw attention through highlighting. You can do this by darkening the surrounding areas or lightening the highlighted areas. Below are three ways.

Highlights for data you create. If you design your own chart or table, highlighting is straightforward. Select the bar, cell, or line to emphasize and highlight it with a color that stands out. Below, the Teachers bar has been converted to black.

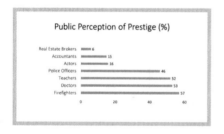
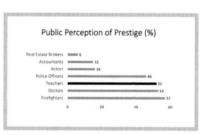

In fact, you may not need any of the labels. It depends on the point you're making. Imagine if I said to a crowd, "Compared with other popular professions, teachers are highly regarded by the public." Then show the following slide:

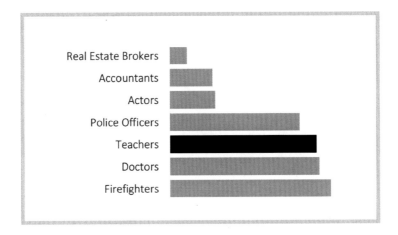

The slide heading simply doesn't matter, since I've already said it out loud. Neither do the numbers and lines—they act as *friction*. With this slide, all the extraneous noise is stripped away.

Highlights for data you cannot modify. What if you want to use a chart or table from a book? Or an old handout? Or maybe you want to copy-and-paste an image you found online? You certainly can't manipulate such charts. If you can't (or don't want to) recreate the data, you can still draw attention to the most important parts.

Say you want to highlight the data on the fifth row, titled Online.

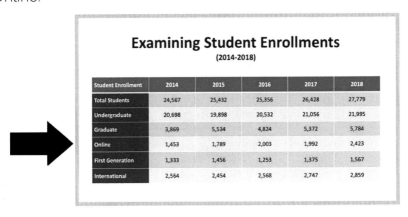

Step 1. Create a solid dark shape (Insert > *Shapes*). It will eventually cover the unnecessary part(s). For this chart, rectangles are needed to cover two areas: the section above the row you want to focus on ("Online") and the section below it.

Step 2. Make the shape slightly transparent, say 40 percent (you can do this under *Format Shape*).

Step 3. Drag the shape(s) and cover the unnecessary part(s) of the chart. Adjust the transparency as necessary so that readers can still see the data underneath, but muted. The uncovered part(s) will automatically stand out.

Examining Student Enrollments
(2014-2018)

Student Enrollment	2014	2015	2016	2017	2018
Total Students	24,567	25,432	25,356	26,428	27,779
Undergraduate	20,698	19,898	20,532	21,056	21,995
Graduate	3,869	5,534	4,824	5,372	5,784
Online	1,453	1,789	2,003	1,992	2,423
First Generation	1,333	1,456	1,253	1,375	1,567
International	2,564	2,454	2,568	2,747	2,859

Using a spotlight. Other times, you may want to call attention to a particular area of the slide, as seen with this medical illustration:

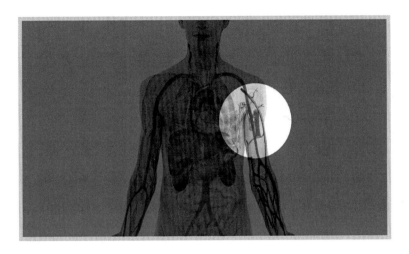

Here, you can create two shapes: 1) a dark, semi-transparent rectangle (as we did with shapes in the previous table), which covers up most of the slide; and 2) a circle that acts as the spotlight. Select both shapes (first the rectangular overlay, then the circle) using your Shift key. Then, *merge* both shapes and *subtract* the circle from the background (*Format > Merge Shapes > Subtract*).

For a step-by-step walk-through, search online using the phrase "How to create a spotlight effect in PowerPoint."[40]

All in all, one of the best things you can do to display data is to *recreate* a simplified version. This does involve some extra effort, but you will get far better results than copying and pasting data or graphs made in Excel or similar spreadsheet programs. In some cases, you may not even *need* a graph! Say you're highlighting one number—for example, the statistic that 79 percent of all online US adults use Facebook. Isn't it more interesting to just show that one figure rather than include respective statistics for Pinterest, Instagram, Weibo, and LinkedIn?

In the end, it's not about the data. It's about the *meaning behind* the data.

PRESENTING. A Challenge: Redesign This Mess!

Let's take a typical slide from a presentation one might see from a textbook publisher. (Generally speaking, they're awful.)

Realism
Roots found in the work of Aristotle 384 – 322 BC

Metaphysical Focus
- Objective order of reality exists regardless of our perception of it.
- Reality consists of two components. They include matter and form, actuality and potentiality

Epistemological Focus
- Observation and investigation of the order of reality (the objects of reality) is the method to obtain knowledge.
- Through sensation of objects of reality, minds acquire data in computer-like fashion.

School Practices
- Education should cultivate rationality. This should occur through the study of organized bodies of knowledge. Disciplines have emerged over time.
- The curriculum should consist of various learned disciplines such as history, geography, language, mathematics, biology, and chemistry. Bodies of knowledge consist of related concepts.
- Teachers should be educated in liberal arts and sciences. Teachers should function as professional educators. Education is teacher centered.

No audience will pay attention to such a dense slide. It simply overwhelms the croc brain. Best-case scenario? Students will dutifully take notes and "deal with it later." (And they won't listen to a word you're saying while they're writing.) Slides like this make for a terrible user experience.

As a presenter, you have a couple of options:
1. Distill and distribute
2. Go back to "first principles"

Let's explore each below.

Option 1: Distill and Distribute (D&D).
There are several problems with this slide:

- Too many ideas being communicated (at least seven)
- The use of full (and multiple) sentences
- The use of formal, academic language
- The lack of visuals (or other supplements to help audience understanding)

Each of these issues acts as friction to the user experience.

First, do we need to include all seven ideas here? Probably not (read: *definitely* not). So take out what's irrelevant and anything that can be mentioned out loud.

Then simplify the wording—as in, make it easy enough for a middle-school child to read. That's where most adults appear to feel comfortable.[41]

The bottom line: *Never, ever use the wording from textbooks or handouts for your slides. They're usually academic and verbose. Always reword to make your slide audience-friendly.* Taking a few minutes to wordsmith existing text will help audiences "get" your slides that much quicker—and remember, those precious seconds can mean the difference between getting it and losing interest.

The bottom line: Never, ever use the wording from textbooks or handouts for your slides. They're usually academic and verbose. Always reword to make your slide audience-friendly.

Here's how I plan to distill this slide:

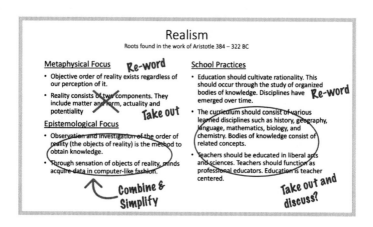

Now to distribute the ideas. One slide will act as the section title, and the other three will communicate ideas related to realism. One idea per slide, with an appropriate visual for each.

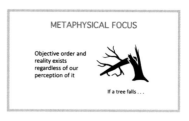
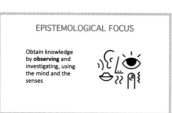
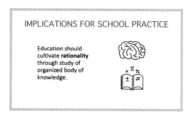

 RESOURCE ALERT: Like the graphic icons from these slides? Check out the FAQ from Chapter 6 for the best sites to download them!

PRO TIP!

Use the finger-snap test to see how quickly audiences will get your slide. Take one slide and show it to someone—a colleague, a friend, or family member. Without context, see if they get it quickly. It shouldn't take more than a few seconds. Anything more—ten seconds?—means you've failed to meet the requirements of the croc brain (i.e., being simple, clear, relevant, and/or novel) and therefore your message will be tuned out. Note: The exception is if you want audiences to spend time analyzing, say, a quote or chart.

Yet, distilling and distributing ideas across multiple slides is often not enough. Why not? Because this assumes that using slides is the best way to communicate. Remember, the purpose of presentation design is to *help audiences get from point A to point B as quickly as possible.*

Here, the goal—reaching point B—is to understand *realism*. What, then, is the best, most efficient way to learn it? Certainly not memorizing a bunch of slides!

This leads us to . . .

Option 2: Go Back to "First Principles."
When most people imagine presenting, they think about using slides. Delivering a speech. Teaching content. Right?

That's the problem. We focus too much on us and what we want to say. We don't think about *them*—the audience— and how *they* receive our information. But effective communication is, as Intel co-founder Andy Grove argued, all about *how well we are understood, not how well we say things.*

It's such a simple concept, but presenters aren't always thinking, *Will audiences understand what I say?* They're too focused on the *What*, not the *How*.

> *How well we communicate is determined not by how well we say things but by how well we are understood.* —Andy Grove, co-founder and former CEO, Intel.

This brings us back to the UX—i.e., *How* your audience interacts with or *experiences* your message. What exactly is the audience going through when seeing that dense slide on realism? Here are some of their likely thoughts:

There's too much information on this slide!
I can't read all this small type.
Let me just copy all this down first . . .
I couldn't care less about all this!
What should I eat for lunch?
I hope we can get a copy of all these slides.

The last thought is symptomatic of the real issue: there's so much going on that students need something to refer back to—or, unfortunately, that some students don't want to do any work. Maybe they don't want to miss anything important and are hoping a copy of the slides will serve as a comprehensive (i.e., "official") outline for the final exam.

Regardless, students here are tuning out. If my goal is to get them to understand realism, what would make for a good UX? Again, let's think from their perspective. If I'm defining the user experience of a student waiting for class to begin, here's what I believe are some of their thoughts:

I hope this presentation isn't boring. And I hope there's a point to learning realism. I'd love to make sense of what I read last night—the concepts are complicated, and I need it clarified and simplified. To be honest, I only skimmed the reading . . . I need the professor to help me grasp the most important stuff. Ideally, they will help me reach an "Aha!" moment. It would also be great if they would help me apply the concepts to real life or, at the very least, understand them well enough to ace the test.

Based on this internal dialogue, this student needs to actively—and deeply—process realism. This slide is screaming for meaning and/or engagement.

And now, it's clear: Our previous attempt to distribute ideas into their own slide is not enough. We need to address that inner student dialogue!

We need to abandon convention. Forget about making incremental improvements or changes to PowerPoint. That's superficial. We need to go back to basics. The fundamentals.

This is the essence of **"first principles" thinking**: stop thinking in terms of incremental improvements based on widely held assumptions, beliefs, and practices (in our case, using PowerPoint as a way to communicate information). Instead, we should question all of it and design solutions from scratch. Going back to the *fundamentals*. Only then can we think more effectively and creatively.

German automobile engineer Karl Benz (of Mercedes-Benz) didn't focus on ways to speed up horse-drawn carriages, the transportation norm of the eighteenth century—that would've limited him to marginal improvements to carriages. Instead, Benz went back to the underlying issue: *getting people from point A to point B faster.* With that in mind, he freed himself from existing constraints to design the first practical automobile.

Modern entrepreneur and business titan Elon Musk similarly applied "first principles" thinking in 2002 in order to send rockets to Mars. Conventional thinking dictated that he buy parts from aerospace manufacturers, which proved to be astronomically expensive. He needed to "boil things down to their fundamental truths, and reason up from there," as he said in a TED interview.[42] What are rockets made of? Aerospace-grade aluminum alloys, titanium, copper, and carbon fiber. Would he need to go through manufacturers to get these materials? What if he bypassed the middleman, created his own company, and purchased raw materials, which were much cheaper? That's exactly what he did when he founded SpaceX.[43]

When you present, think about what Benz and Musk did. Ask yourself, *What am I trying to accomplish? What does the audience get out of all this? Is this topic even important? How do I get the audience to that "Aha!" moment?*

All of a sudden, the cosmetic changes everyone talks about—fixing fonts, colors, and the such—seem trivial.

Let's start by answering some fundamental questions.

Questions	Possible Answers
Is this topic even important enough to bring up?	This depends on what you believe will help students most.
What are we really trying to accomplish with this slide?	I want students to truly understand realism and how it relates to their future career as teachers.

Questions	Possible Answers
Who are we serving?	Students who want to see a point in all this while juggling so many other things.
What's the best way to accomplish our goal?	Get students involved—to actively and deeply process the concept of realism.

Think about the purpose of teaching realism (or whatever topic you teach). Remember the student's internal dialogue? Why are they learning realism? Is it important to your curriculum? If not, then remove realism as a topic.

Wow . . . we have potentially killed a piece of content. Now we're a step closer to fulfilling one of our main roles as presenter: *to curate information.*[44] No more dumping content onto slides. That's for amateurs.

However, if realism is important, then let's go back to the *Why.* In Chapter 2, you learned to create a one-sentence takeaway. Here is the template again:

> **By the end of the presentation, audiences will be able to [know or do XYZ], so that [their lives will be improved in XYZ way].**

The last part answers the *Why*—the purpose:

> *By the end of the lecture, students will be able to explain how realism as a philosophy (compared to idealism) affects the current education approach,* **so that they can appreciate why schools today focus so much on accountability and standardized testing.**

This is another reason why developing a one-sentence takeaway is important—as a reminder to you, the presenter, what the point of all this is. If the purpose is to "appreciate why schools today focus so much on accountability and standardized testing," then we need to talk about how realism shapes the current education approach. We're *Connecting*—the first C in the acronym CIA (refer back to Chapter 3).

So instead of a boring, abstract definition of realism, I start with a concrete hook:

"Class, what's more important—schools that prepare us for the workforce or schools that fulfill our intellectual potential?"

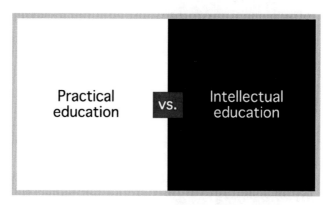

Notice I don't open with the term *realism* (or its counterpart *idealism*) by saying something like "Today we'll focus on how realism as a philosophy shaped modern education . . ." That would guarantee a negative UX. But by discussing the pros/cons of a practical, skills-based education versus one focused on developing the intellect, students will start to see relevance in their own lives. *Exactly* what the croc brain needs.

The best part of this opening hook? *You technically don't even need a slide for this.* Just ask the question out loud. If you really want a slide, the above is one option. Or if you really want to emphasize your opening, then fine, put up the question, like this:

> ## What's more important:
> ## a practical **education**
> ## or an intellectual **education?**

A bit wordier, but light years ahead of the original, dense-heavy slide. Now students are involved.

Let's stop for a minute. Think about one topic *you* teach, whether it's related to science, business management, literature, history, nursing, or whatever.

Is it a theory? A problem? A how-to?

Now think about a concrete opening hook that helps students see the usefulness of your topic. Forget the actual terms and vocabulary or any of the technical stuff. How can you turn that topic into something students will care about? That's *Connecting*.

Next, the *Instruction* (the "I" in CIA). Here's where you go into the lecture. The terms. The heavy lifting, so to speak. After discussing the pros and cons of a practical versus intellectual education, you might transition into the instruction by saying:

"The current focus on job skills is actually rooted in Aristotle's work. You're probably thinking, 'How are the two possibly related?' Let's start by exploring two philosophies: *realism* and *idealism* . . ."

Now it's appropriate to discuss terms and specifics. The audience learns better when you anchor new knowledge with something familiar—in this case, the current education approach.

The audience learns better when you anchor new knowledge with something familiar.

Students have more context to understand terms like *realism, metaphysics,* and *idealism.* They aren't sitting in a vacuum. Now they're more receptive to the technical stuff. Here's where I might use the slides from Option 1:

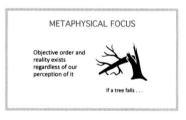

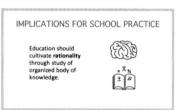

I might add a quote or two and get students involved. More importantly, I recommend interspersing the lecture with student involvement, whether via questions or group work. One activity I absolutely love is stop–jot–share, the learning technique described in Chapter 4. It helps students actively retrieve information that's been presented.

With stop–jot–share, students get a chance to write down everything that's been discussed in their notes—a summary of sorts that can help them for the final exam. Furthermore, you won't feel as much of a need to provide a copy of your slide deck.

Here's a BEFORE (original slide) and AFTER (a redesigned version) below. Note the left side is the slide, and the plan of action is on the right):

BEFORE:

LECTURE
(20 minutes)
Go over everything in this slide
("Let's talk about realism today and how it impacted . . .")

AFTER:

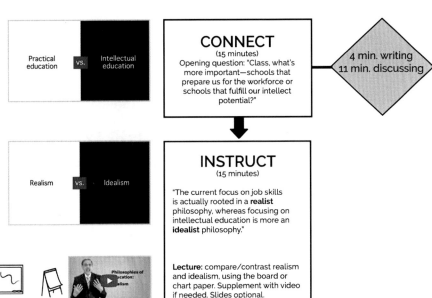

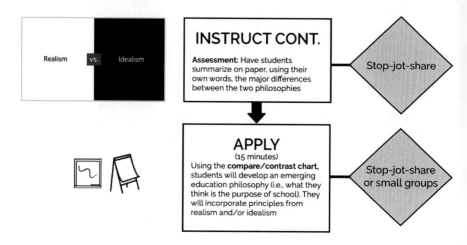

As you can imagine, there are many ways to teach students about realism. Other ideas include having students analyze videos, articles, and quotes.

Notice a few things?

First, the new way takes longer to present. But this isn't a problem—if the idea is worth teaching, it will take time. Otherwise, don't include it in your PowerPoint. Learning is a *sense-making process*. Give audiences time to "struggle" with the content.

Second, notice that slides play a secondary role to your purpose—as they should. CIA focuses on what would get students from point A (not knowing) to point B (knowing). Everything else acts as support (just as visuals do for the narrator in a documentary).

> **Learning is a *sense-making* process. Give audiences time to "struggle" with the content.**

Finally, see how interaction (the stuff in the diamond) plays a big role? It's incorporated into the beginning, middle, and end. Getting audiences to participate regularly should be part of your new "normal."

PRESENTING. THE BOTTOM LINE

Good design was never about making slides pretty.

It's about reducing the friction to understanding and learning.

It's about improving the overall user experience, the UX.

In many cases, simply distilling your ideas and distributing them across multiple slides will fix a lot of your PowerPoint problems.

But real design goes beyond cosmetic. Questioning assumptions and conventions are more important.

What if simply showing a title and three bullet points is not the best way to communicate your point? What if a photograph, a quotation, a story, or an activity works better?

Now you're removing conventional constraints and developing solutions from scratch, just as innovators and "first principles" thinkers do.

Real design goes back to the fundamentals and solves problems.

When you do that, you create the *ultimate* user experience.

[33]We often overestimate what audiences know, because what's new to them is often basic to us. This "expert blind spot" is a major reason why presenters (and teachers) lose their audiences. Furthermore, the more knowledge one accumulates, the more he or she should beware of this phenomenon. I frequently have to check myself to see if I've assumed too much about my audience's existing knowledge of a topic.

[34]Note, however, that when an audience has "bought into" the premise of your message—as students might listening to your inside scoop to landing a great job—you can get more detailed. They'll listen and work through your slides once the initial message makes it past the gatekeeper and into the rationally thinking part—the neocortex. Staying engrossed in a ninety-minute podcast or a three-hundred-page book therefore won't be a problem. At the same time, don't overstay your welcome; an invitation to continue doesn't give you license to keep talking or stuff your slide with content. Staying attuned is part of the challenge.

[35]Nina Kim also advised and designed this book as well.

[36]Think of the micro type used in the legal disclosures of print pharmaceutical ads. Its size indicates it's not meant to be read. The lower level of importance explains why footnotes tend to use smaller type sizes.

[37]A case can be made to distill the on-screen text even more. Perhaps there's some friction in having to read the entire sentence. Here, I try to remember marketer Seth Godin's (n.d.) golden rule: No more than six words per slide. Hard to do? Sure, but not impossible.

[38]The latter is part of the 10/20/30 rule popularized by marketer Guy Kawasaki: Have no more than ten slides, speak for no more than twenty minutes, and make sure the type size is at least thirty points. (For the record, the number of slides doesn't matter; it's what you do with them that counts.)

[39]In marketing and advertising parlance, the "hero shot" refers informally to the main or most important visual that represents your brand/product. On a website page, the hero shot is often the first and largest photo that readers see as they scroll.

[40]ShapeChef has a step-by-step process here: https://www.shapechef.com/blog/how-to-create-a-spotlight-effect-in-powerpoint

[41]See Snow (2015), who tested the reading grade level of some of the most popular books of all time, including J.K. Rowling's Harry Potter and the Sorcerer's Stone (~5th – 6th grade) and Ernest Hemingway's The Old Man and the Sea (4th grade).

[42]See https://youtu.be/0JQXoSmC1rs (Malek, 2016)

[43]For details, watch Musk's thinking process as explained by Steve Jurvetson, partner at Silicon Valley venture firm DFJ (Draper Fisher

Jurvetson): **https://youtu.be/3aXNWGwis4w** (DraperTV, 2015).
[44]Other than curating content, the other major role presenters play is to design experiences that help the audience understand what you're communicating. For teachers, this may be learning experiences such as group work, class discussions, and class debates. For conference presenters, this may be case studies, anecdotes, Q&A, surveys, and other ways to make information more concrete or get audiences to engage. Curating content and designing learning experiences lay at the heart of Option 2.

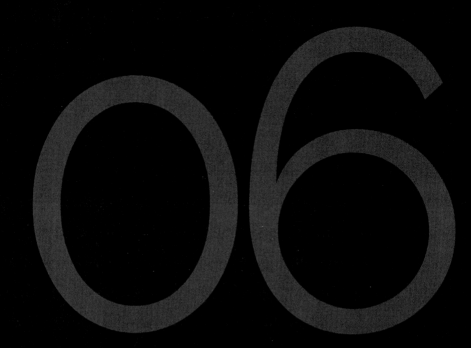

06

FREQUENTLY ASKED
QUESTIONS

Q. I have way too much to cover. I can't just focus on one message as you recommend—what should I do?

A. First, it's critical to remind yourself how the human brain works. The fact is, it finds ways to ignore messages—particularly if they are boring, irrelevant, unclear, or simply too much—so that it can conserve calories and save energy. Because of this, your average audience member will lose focus after fifteen to twenty minutes.

But I understand that at times presenters have no choice but to cover a lot; without the full amount of content, students/attendees cannot move forward. For example, my education undergrads have to pass a rigorous teacher-performance assessment (called the Educative Teacher Performance Assessment, or edTPA) to get their license. It involves four tasks, divided into eighteen subtasks, requiring candidates to plan lessons, videotape their teaching, analyze students' work, and so forth. Each subtask has its own requirements regarding page length, format, etc. I, as presenter, have to give students a breakdown of the whole damn thing—step-by-step: *What do you do first? Second? Third? Last?*

You probably have something similar. Maybe you have to explain all the nerves and muscles in the human body, the inner workings of a combustion engine, or how a balance sheet works. And you know there's simply no getting around it.

First, remember the D&D rule from Chapter 5 (i.e., *Distill* and *Distribute*). We must always strive to develop one idea per slide, rather than several. Fine—what else? you ask.

If the audience has some background on the topic—for example, they read a chapter on the nervous system last week—then begin the presentation by activating their prior knowledge. Don't jump into lecturing just yet, as that would instantly turn students into passive learners.

How do you activate prior knowledge? Any number of ways will work. Here are two ways I do this:

Method #1: Affinity Mapping. I have students create an *affinity map*, a project-management technique where groups of four to five students write down everything they know (or remember) about a topic on sticky notes. For instance, if the topic is the nervous system, students may decide to jot down terms like *brain, spinal cord*, and *nerves*. They may even write down pieces of information like "The spinal cord is responsible for transmitting information via nerve impulses to the brain." Sticky notes can then be grouped by categories like *central nervous system* and *peripheral nervous system.* (It's up to students to define these groups.)[45]

Priming students through a retrieval and sense-making process allows them to better grasp the content.

Method #2: K-W-L Chart. A popular grade-school technique, K-W-Ls encourage audiences to activate their prior knowledge of a topic and take ownership of their learning. K-W-L stands for:

What You **K**now
What You **W**ant to Know
What You **L**earned

Let's say nursing students need to know the four-step

nursing process to ensure the quality of patient care—i.e., the *assessment phase*, the *diagnosing phase*, the *planning phase*, and the *implementing phase*. Slides are an efficient tool here; before you present, however, start with a K-W-L chart. First, ask them what they already *Know* (the "K" in the K-W-L). This can be done in small groups or as a class. Write students' responses on the board. Then ask them what they *Want* to know (the "W") regarding that topic: questions, wonderings, etc.

Examples:
What am I allowed (and not allowed) to ask patients?
Can I talk with others about my experiences with patients?
What if a patient argues and becomes belligerent?

Isn't this much better than jumping right into the presentation? Now students have a stake—ownership—in their learning. Only at the end will students address the "L" from the K-W-L, by summarizing what they *Learned* about the nursing process.

Affinity mapping and K-W-L charts are just two ways to address content-heavy presentations. As long as you prime audiences upfront, they will be more receptive to the lecture.

But what if your audience comes in cold, with little background knowledge? I'm betting they will still be able to contribute upfront. Even with pitches or, say, an introduction to new technology at a conference, you can find ways to involve the audience. Maybe start by asking about problems or issues they encounter related to your pitch or solution. Here's where you earn your keep. Get creative. How can you set up the audience—and yourself—for success?

Make every presentation less about "disseminating information" and more about *connecting*. Building a dialogue. That's powerful communication!

As for the presentation itself, here are **five** other recommendations to improve the user experience when you simply must deliver lots of content. (I assume at this point you have already done your best to distill the content from each slide and distribute them across multiple slides—the D&D rule described last chapter.)

1. At the start, **include an agenda** of major topics covered as a preview. Attendees hate *not* knowing how much you cover. Part of communicating effectively is the ability to manage expectations. If possible, provide the agenda separately and beforehand (perhaps via a handout or written on the side of the board, or even as the first slide audiences see as they walk in), so that you can jump right into the opening hook. You don't want to waste the precious first few minutes (where audience attention is at its highest) by "going over" what you're about to present: "OK, let's start with today's agenda . . ." Nope.

2. For each new section of your presentation, **use "roadmaps"** so audiences get a sense of where you are. Roadmaps help audiences see the forest (the big picture) beyond the trees (the details). It also addresses the "Are we almost done yet?" question that invariably creeps up during content-heavy sessions.

In the two examples below, notice how the word *Assessing* is highlighted in black, whereas the rest of the words are set in gray.

Two ways to show audiences they are entering the third section
of the presentation

3. Every ten minutes or so, **break up the monotony by involving the audience** in some way, whether through activities or even simply asking them questions. I prefer those which involve *every* attendee, not just a few. Quizzes are one the best ways to do this, especially when you ask audiences to respond using their digital devices (smartphone, tablet, or laptop). See Chapter 4 on using Quizlet or Pear Deck. When I conduct workshops on teaching, I have faculty members apply the content to their own classroom for every major topic I present. And then they share.

4. For each point you present, **relate back to the *Why***, as in *Why does it matter?* The one-sentence takeaway from Chapter 2 should help. If I present an education theory, for instance, I connect that theory to how it helps my students become effective teachers. Tying back to the purpose is even more critical with content-heavy presentations. Yet most presenters don't talk about this until the very end. That's a big mistake, considering how often the audience's brains tunes out. As presenters, we have to constantly remind the audience why they're there. Relate to the *Why* regularly—in every slide, if appropriate.

5. **Build anticipation** for something that comes at the end. In one of my education lectures, I told students, "As we go over the details of the teaching profession, think about why you want to become a teacher. At the end, you'll have

a chance to post your thoughts on Twitter!" In this way, you've said something unexpected and/or intriguing that gets audiences to invest in your presentation while enticing them to remain engaged—a kind of suspended hook!

I'm not necessarily talking about prizes and other gimmicks that offer little incentive to listen to the actual presentation.

It's better to provide tips, secrets, and other hacks to help attendees leverage your content. And, yes, technically the "threat" of giving students a quiz at the end of class will keep students' attention, but it won't build positive anticipation. (As a rule, I use quizzes informally to check in on students, not as a way to hold their attention hostage.) The better choice is to use something they will find helpful.

Q. Should I give audiences a copy of my slide deck (i.e., a leave-behind)?

A. It's possible your students expect a copy of your lecture/presentation. Maybe the conference requires you to upload a copy to their website, or maybe you want everyone to have one.

As a general rule, I try not to provide a copy of my slide deck. You know, the ones that look like these:

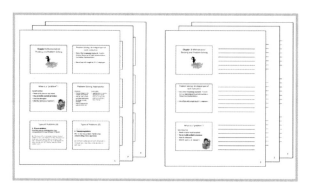

I know it's hard *not* to provide leave-behinds. I still do it sometimes. But if you've done your PowerPoint right—meaning you're using lots of visuals and minimal text, as in a documentary—then providing a copy is meaningless. Especially to those who weren't present to hear you speak. Who would ever understand a bunch of pictures? That's what I tell audiences at my workshops.

Remember the Redundancy Test from the Introduction of this book: If your slide deck is basically your lecture, then you've failed. The best ones cannot stand on their own—they merely support you. *You* are the star attraction.

> **If you've done your PowerPoints right—meaning you're using lots of visuals and minimal text, as in a documentary—then providing a copy is meaningless.**

The goal is for students (or audiences in general) to learn, take notes, reflect—i.e., make sense of things—during your presentation. They're not passive recipients of information, waiting for your notes so they can parrot them for the final exam.

But if you *have* to give a content-heavy presentation, a content-heavy slide deck is inevitable. Go ahead, then. Give copies of your slide deck. They're going to need the reference. You have my permission.

But I would add one critical caveat: If you give audiences a leave-behind, make sure they have an opportunity to retrieve that information. Especially if they're students.

In other words, don't just give content and be done with it. That encourages passive learning—the kind students will instantly forget. Instead, have them repeat (or paraphrase) that information during the course of the presentation. This means after ten to fifteen minutes of lecturing/presenting, ask students to write down everything that was just discussed, to summarize it. This forces them to retrieve information from their brain—an important learning process discussed in Chapter 4. I recommend the stop–jot–share technique.

Again, **try to avoid giving audiences your slide deck.** I would prefer you provide a one to three paragraph summary of the presentation as a leave-behind (i.e., a slightly more detailed abstract). This is perfect for conferences and meetings. And it discourages students from missing class just because they can always read the slides later on.

The alternative is to provide an outline of the major topics you discuss with blank spaces for note-taking during the actual presentation. I like the Cornell method of taking notes,[46] which encourages students to pull out key ideas and summarize the lecture, as this template to the right illustrates.

STOP AND WATCH

For a primer on how to take Cornell notes, watch this short video (5:26): **https://youtu.be/ WtWglyE04OQ**

I actually make it a point to teach students, particularly first- or second-year undergraduates, how to take notes.

Why? When students are forced to "retrieve" information—by summarizing, repeating, or paraphrasing what has been presented—you improve the odds that the content sticks. Retrieval practice, a popular technique discussed in Chapter 4, is critical when you cover lots of information. If you feel compelled to give students a copy of the slide deck, pair it with regular opportunities for retrieval practice (at least twice a session).

Q. All these suggestions are great, but I have no time to make my slides "viewer-friendly." What can I do?

A. On the one hand, it's easy for me to tell you to invest time in your slides if you want engaged audiences. And it's true. However, the bigger question is: *Do you have to use slides?* Is it required, or are you simply following convention? Sometimes other non-slide methods are better. A discussion, for instance, can be equally as effective, provided you give students an outline for note-taking. Remember, some of the best presentations don't use slides (see Ken Robinson's TED Talk, mentioned in Chapter 1).

Audiences, particularly those within a classroom setting, can often be better served without slides. Same with faculty at department meetings. The point is to question conventional wisdom and put audience engagement first.

For busy professors, the most efficient way to design slides is to create a summary and outline first, as I've shown in Chapters 2 and 3, which focus on what you want audiences to come away with, and then design a way of making sure that happens—it could be with slides; it could be without.

Don't get stuck on convention. (And never use slide templates!)

Q. Where can I get high-quality, royalty-free visuals for my slides?

A. Most of us probably just search for images in Google (or other search engines). Yet most of those images are not public domain or creative-commons licensed, meaning they are protected by copyright law. Copyright owners can ask you to remove the photo or even sue you (however unlikely). If you're using the photos for commercial reasons, then you *definitely* need to be careful. Consult a lawyer if necessary.

As a general rule, assume that any image you find on the internet is covered by copyright. Many stock photography websites, however, grant what's called a *creative-commons* (CC) *license*, which means as long as you follow their rules (such as giving credit to the creator of the image somewhere on your slides or linking the image to the owner's website), you should be able to use their picture.

For Google Images, you can filter your searches to only look for images that are labeled for reuse.

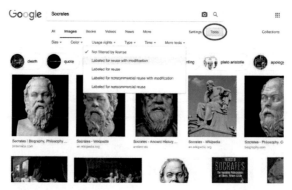

When searching for pictures of Socrates, I click on Tools (circled) > Usage rights > Labeled for reuse with modification (select whichever filter fits your need)

You can do the same with websites like Flickr.com, which I also recommend as a photograph repository.

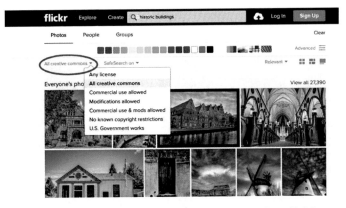

With photos on Flickr.com, filter your images by clicking on
Any license (upper left hand corner) > All creative commons

An alternative is an aggregator site like search. creativecommons.org. There, you can enter your search query and it will comb through Google Images, Flickr, Pixabay, and other image sites to find creative-commons licensed pictures. You can even add *CC Search* to your web browser.

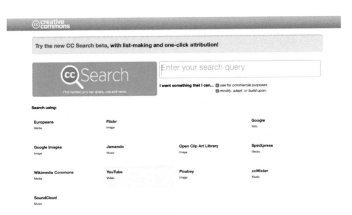

The creative commons search page
(https://search.creativecommons.org)

But there are other free sites that offer royalty-free images of high quality. Unsplash (unsplash.com) is one of them. Others include Canva Photos (canva.com/photos/free) and Free Images (Freeimages.com or Freeimages.co.uk).

The Library of Congress also offers lots of high-quality (and "old-school") pictures that are public domain, which means anyone can use them. A tremendous resource. Topics range widely, from bridges to holidays to jazz to presidential portraits.

The websites above are simply my recommendation for photos that look a little more inspired than the ones we often see in poorly designed websites and brochures.

Aside from stock photos, consider using *graphic icons*, those little black-and-white symbols representing . . . well, everything. Anything you could want. Icons strip away all the potential distractions of photos. Say you want to display a smartphone in your slide. A photo may show a particular brand of smartphone that may simply add to the cognitive load, with all its apps. Using icons can streamline the user experience.

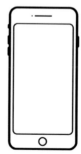

Photograph of a smartphone
(by Sara Kurfeß on Unsplash)

A simple graphic icon
of a smartphone

Microsoft PowerPoint has graphic icons built in as of 2018, which is long overdue (go to *Insert > Icons*). Just make sure you update to their latest version. You can choose from categories like technology, communication, education, arrows, art, food and drink, and more (see examples below). You can even change icon colors and resize them. Just know that PowerPoint's choices of icons are limited. What if you want an icon representing, say, *equality* or *community?*

You can find graphic icons on many websites, like Icons8 (Icons8.com), or Flat Icon (flaticon.com), or *The Noun Project* (thenounproject.com). However, there are limitations. Some sites will only allow you to download icons in lower pixels (e.g., 24 or 96 px), which is fine for most slides. Other sites require author attribution, which means you have to credit the author/creator with a link on your slides. Still others limit the icon color you can download to black.

But again, for most slide presentations (particularly those given in the classroom), these limitations aren't a big deal.

If you want more flexibility, however, you can always pay. I use graphic icons not only in my slides, but also in assignment handouts, my syllabi, website, conference posters, and books. If you have wider needs like me, I recommend choosing the premium model (i.e., subscribing for access on a monthly or annual basis).

If you need flexibility with your graphic icons, I recommend The Noun Project. It has millions to choose from, it's easy to navigate, and it's only US$20/year for educators as of 2019 (normally $40/year).

**Graphic icons at The Noun Project
(https://thenounproject.com)**

Q. What are the best fonts to use in slides?

A. Readability is the most important criteria, according to instructional designer Nina Kim (our guest expert in Chapter 5). As such, avoid decorative fonts like Papyrus or Brush Script and those that are overused (e.g., Comics Sans, Arial, and Times New Roman).

You might want to also consider whether to use *serif* or *sans serif* fonts. Serif fonts have small lines or extensions at the end of the letter, which gives them a more traditional look (see circled below). Popular serif fonts include Times New Roman, Georgia, and Baskerville. *Sans serif* fonts, on the other hand, have an unadorned look, which makes it appear cleaner and more modern. Popular ones include Arial, Helvetica, Calibri, and Lucida Grande.

$\mathcal{S}\text{erif}$ Sans Serif

There's debate about which one is more readable, which can impact the user experience. Some think the "feet" of the serif make each letter distinct, whereas others believe the extra flourishes can impede readability at smaller sizes. If you were an audience member sitting at the back of the room, which of the below would be slightly easier to absorb?

Reality consists of two components: matter and form, and actuality and potentiality.	Reality consists of two components: matter and form, and actuality and potentiality.

Two commonly used fonts in PowerPoint:
Times New Roman (serif font) at left,
and Calibri (sans serif) at right. Which slide is easier to read?

I prefer sans serif fonts, as does Nina. They're modern and popular today. Other fonts available in Microsoft Office that she recommends include Century Gothic, Franklin Gothic, and Trebuchet.

Q. How should I title my presentation?

A. When audiences walk in and see your opening slide, the UX (user experience) officially begins. You want your opening title to intrigue, to build anticipation. Even if your topic is *mitosis*. You know who writes great titles? Marketers and journalists. Getting and holding attention is part of their job, since 55 percent of online users spend fewer than fifteen seconds actively on a web page.[47] Engagement is a perennial challenge, and it starts with a captivating title. Here are three ways to do this.

Phrase the title as a question. A question automatically draws people in, because it's got to be answered! The best ones, however, tap into what people are already thinking—"joining the conversation already happening in the customer's head," as marketers say. That connection gives you the advantage. All the resistance or skepticism (which is sometimes the case when students feel forced to attend classes) melts away.

One of my clients, Michelle, an accounting instructor, recalled how she originally titled her presentation *Tax Credits and Tax Deductions,* which, admittedly, is fairly boring. By simply rephrasing the topic as a question (*What's the Difference Between Tax Credits and Tax Deductions?*), Michelle potentially taps into our insecurities about taxes— namely that we wished we knew more. Furthermore, she creates an expectation for an answer. In this way, questions create focus.

Use how-to's. Some of the most-read articles online are "how-to" articles (e.g., *How to Earn Passive Income, How to Spend Less While Traveling,* etc.). They tap into our desire to improve ourselves. How can you improve your audience's lives? Titles like *How to Improve the Quality of Your Patients' Care* (as opposed to the straightforward title *Patient Care*) or *How to Write a Résumé that Gets Employers to Call You Back* (rather than *Résumé Writing 101*) can intrigue and capture attention.

Employ lists. People love to read "listicles" (e.g., *20 Ways to Earn More Money, The 5 Vegetables You Need to Eat,* etc.). Maybe it's because they cut through all the fluff and just "give it to you straight." The best listicle headlines, of course, relate to something the audience cares about. In academic presentations, there are plenty of opportunities to employ lists: *Which of These 9 Forms of Intelligence Do You Have? The 5 Dimensions of Personality that Shape Your Life.* Wherever possible, provide value in the headline.

Q. Any final (awesome) tips that will polish my presentation?

A. Yes. First, try **Presentation View**. While you should *practice, practice, practice* your speech (more about this later), use *Presentation View* if you have a lot to remember. This mode allows you—and not the audience—to see the upcoming slide, elapsed time, and notes. All on your laptop. It saved my life as a new lecturer, especially when I didn't have time to practice! I still use *Presentation View* once in a while, although my default approach now is to practice my speech until it becomes second nature. You can find *Presenter View* under the *Slide Show* tab.

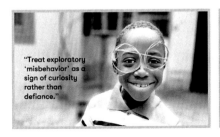 

With Presenter View, audiences see only the slide (left), whereas on your computer you see the current slide, the next one, your notes, and more (right)

Second, invest in a **clicker**. Trust me—it's like night and day. Think again of the user experience. When you're stuck behind a podium, audiences forget you're there, since they are focusing on the slides. As such, you lose stage presence, a critical part of effective communication.

I use the *Beboncool Wireless Remote Presentation USB*

clicker, but there are many options to choose from. They will change your game.

Finally, practice your presentation by **scripting** your speech. Yes, literally write out the whole thing—not just bulleted notes on index cards. While some people [think they] are good at delivering off the cuff, most of us benefit by rehearsing *a lot* and memorizing. And much has to do with getting the timing right. I write out how I introduce myself (during conferences and workshops, for instance), my jokes, and even informal language (e.g., "gonna" instead of "going to"; "shouldn't" instead of "should not"; and the occasional well-timed use of the word "shit").

Teleprompter apps like iPrompt Pro and Teleprompter+ 3 may help, but honestly, nothing beats plain old practice and memorization. It's the not-so-secret secret to powerful communication and presentations.

---

[45]For a step-by-step procedure of affinity mapping, read my article at https://normaneng.org/reviewing-for-finals-try-affinity-mapping/ (Eng, 2018, December 10)
[46]Developed by Walter Pauk at Cornell University (see Pauk & Owens, 2013)
[47]See: http://time.com/12933/what-you-think-you-know-about-the-web-is-wrong/ (Haile, 2014)

CHAPTER SUMMARIES

CHAPTER-BY-CHAPTER SUMMARY.

Here you'll find the book's distilled highlights, including a short summary, excerpted quotes, pro tips, and videos—all in one easy-to-find place.

Enjoy.

Chapter 1.
YOUR MINDSET.

KEY INSIGHT.
Think of PowerPoint as documentaries.

SUMMARY.
Your presentation goal (and approach) is to get your message through in the shortest possible time by thinking of PowerPoints as documentaries.

VIDEO 1.
Watch the preview of Ken Burn's documentary The Civil War (1:03). See how the narration and visuals integrate into a seamless learning experience?
https://youtu.be/IztrtVmthfM

VIDEO 2.

Watch Sir Ken Robinson's "Do Schools Kill Creativity?" TED Talks speech without slides, which has been viewed over 53,000,000 times—one of the most popular presentations of all time.
https://youtu.be/iG9CE55wbtY

Chapter 2.
YOUR MESSAGE.

KEY INSIGHT.
Create a "one-sentence takeaway."

SUMMARY.
When defining your main message, figure out Why people need to hear that message. That's what people care about. Without addressing it, you will sound like every other presenter.

KEY QUOTES.
Teaching is not about "covering." It's about "uncovering."

The textbook is responsible for covering everything. You're responsible for magnifying the most important parts.

ONE-SENTENCE TAKEAWAY TEMPLATE.

By the end of the presentation, audiences will be able to [know or do XYZ], so that [their lives will be improved in XYZ way].

PRO TIP.

With classroom presentations, add a How to your one-sentence takeaway. This answers the question, How will your students learn the content? This is the method, strategy, activity, or tool you want students to use.

For instance: Students will be able to evaluate the credibility of online sources (the What) by using the "triangulation" method (the How), so that they make better buying decisions (the Why).

The How specifies the actual learning that takes place.

Here, the "one-sentence takeaway" evolves into more of a "one-sentence lesson plan." It crystallizes the three most important parts of your presentation: 1) What students need to know (or do); 2) How they will learn this; and 3) Why they ought to learn this. Chapter 4 helps you flesh out your How.

Chapter 3.
YOUR OUTLINE.

KEY INSIGHT.
Start your presentation with the Why.

SUMMARY.
The Why—the purpose—is your new way to open presentations. When planning your outline, the first question you ask is: Why am I presenting [Topic XYZ]?

Your answer informs the opening. Find that hook! Once it is established, the content will follow. This approach may radically depart from the way you used to present, but your audience will be immediately engaged. You want them to reach that moment of clarity—that "Aha!" moment, as presentation expert Jerry Weissman calls it.

But that won't happen when logic is employed at the start. The audience's primitive croc brains simply won't allow it. Get past that gatekeeper by being novel, simple, clear, and relevant. Connect, Instruct, then Apply.

KEY QUOTES.
Ineffective presenters fail because they communicate with the highly developed part of their brain (reasoning and logic) even though audiences receive the message using their primitive brain (fight or flight).

Relating your takeaway message to your audience's lives at the beginning is the single most effective way to 10X your presentation.

Your big revelation up front will sustain the rest of your presentation.

In a classroom, I highly recommend asking a question or posing a scenario as your opening hook. Both require students to get involved immediately.

Of the twenty things you want to cover today, students won't remember more than a few.

PRO TIP.
If you pose a scenario (or anything longer than a sentence), don't post it on the slide and read it to the audience. They lose focus as their eyes and ears compete to read and listen at the same time. Do one or the other. Verbalize the scenario out loud (yes, memorize what you're going to say)

or post the text on the slide and stay silent as the audience reads it to themselves.

Chapter 4
YOUR INTERACTION.

KEY INSIGHT.
Insert audience interaction every ten minutes.

SUMMARY.
When planning the content part of your presentation, think about involving every single audience member in some way. That's the gold standard for participation. The rules shouldn't change even for conference presentations. Asking attendees to raise their hands for an informal survey or dividing into small groups to discuss their thoughts about a topic and then sharing with the rest of the audience (much as students would in a turn-and-talk) can liven any presentation. Even if it's focused on research.

KEY QUOTE.
The standard for effective classroom participation isn't to get some students to talk. It should be to get everyone actively involved.

PRO TIP.
Use turn-and-talk when students aren't raising their hands. Sometimes I'll ask a question, realize that no one wants to participate, and say, "You know what? Work out the answer with a partner." More hands will go up afterward, as students are better prepared.

Chapter 5
YOUR DESIGN.

KEY INSIGHT.
Consider the user experience (UX).

SUMMARY.
Good design should never be about making slides "pretty."
It's about reducing the friction to understanding and
learning; it's about improving the overall user experience.
In many cases, simply distilling your ideas and distributing
them across multiple slides will fix a majority of your
PowerPoint problems.

Real design goes beyond cosmetic. Questioning
assumptions and conventions are more important. What if
simply showing a title and three bullet points is not the best
way to communicate your point? What if a photograph,
a quotation, a story, or an activity works better? Now
you're removing conventional constraints and developing
solutions from scratch—just as innovators and "first
principles" thinkers do.

Real design goes back to the fundamentals and solves
problems. When you do that, you create the ultimate user
experience.

KEY QUOTES.
Every time you present, you create a user experience—
whether you intend to or not.

The goal of design is to help audiences get from point A
to point B as quickly as possible. Removing the "friction" in
your slides is one way to do this.

"Distill" and "distribute" (D&D) are the two most effective
design principles to instantly simplify and improve the way

audiences respond to you.

People learn better from graphics and narration than from graphics, narration, and on-screen text.

How well we communicate is determined not by how well we say things but by how we are understood. — Andy Grove, cofounder and former CEO, Intel.

The audience learns better when you anchor new knowledge to something familiar.

Learning is a sense-making process. Give audiences time to "struggle" with the content.

PRO TIPS.
When using visuals, fill the whole slide with the image. Go borderless. Images then become the "hero." It sounds obvious, but non-designers often don't think to do that. They subordinate the image to the text, which often leaves it as an afterthought. Think of visuals used in documentaries.

Use the Eyedropper tool to match colors in your slide. That sense of cohesion reduces the friction and improves the user experience. To learn how to use the Eyedropper tool, search online with the phrase "Use Eyedropper to match colors on your slide" or check the support site for Microsoft Office (support.office.com).

Consider removing your slide headings or making them smaller. It's interesting how PowerPoint (and others) default to having a heading in each slide. Its large size suggests it's really important! Yet the body is often more important and it should therefore be upgraded, from a visual hierarchy perspective. Ask yourself, Is the heading even necessary? Use the "finger-snap test" to see how quickly audiences will get your slide. Take one slide and show it to someone—a colleague, a friend, or a family member. Without context, will they get it quickly? (It shouldn't take more than three seconds.)

REFLECT.
Do all these changes actually matter? Maybe these tweaks don't mean much to you. All that time and effort for what? It's the content that matters, right?

When you present in front of industry experts, it's easier to stuff content. Their knowledge is more sophisticated compared with novices, so presenters can afford to go heavier on the content. This may explain why professors teaching advanced biochemistry, for instance, may feel that design and visual flourishes are a waste of time, that graduate-level students or conference attendees don't require such visual "crutches."

Yet cognitive overload is a universal phenomenon. Same with user experience. All messages are still received by the primitive fight-or-flight brain. It still pays to be simple, novel, and concrete.

In the end, changing the type size from 28-point to 40-point may not mean much on its own (although the audience member in the back of the room may appreciate it), but combined with other design principles—namely simplicity, composition, and relationships—the collective user experience will improve.

It's like being nice. One time won't make an impression, but if done consistently, people will generally see you that way. As such, design matters tremendously.]

Chapter 6
FREQUENTLY ASKED QUESTIONS.

KEY QUOTE.
If you've done your PowerPoint right—meaning you're using lots of visuals and minimal text, as in a documentary—then providing a copy of it is meaningless.

VIDEO.
For a primer on how to take Cornell notes, watch this short video (5:26): https://youtu.be/WtW9IyE04OQ

RECOMMENDATION.
If you need flexibility with your graphic icons, I recommend The Noun Project. It has millions to choose from, it's easy to navigate, and it's only US$20/year for educators as of 2019 (normally $40/year).

REFERENCES.

Anonymous. (2004). The harder hard sell [Special report: The future of advertising]. *The Economist*. Retrieved from https://www.economist.com/special-report/2004/06/24/the-harder-hard-sell

Bacon, D.R., and Stewart, K.A. (2006). How fast do students forget what they learn in consumer behavior? A longitudinal study. *Journal of Marketing Education*, *28*(3), 181-192. https://doi.org/10.1177/0273475306291463.

Brown, P.C., Roediger III, H.L., and McDaniel, M.A. (2014). *Make it stick: The science of successful learning*. *Cambridge*, MA: Belknap Press.

Bunce, D.M., Flens, E.A., and Neiles, K.Y. (2010). How long can students pay attention in class? A study of student attention decline using clickers. *Journal of Chemical Education*, *87*(12), 1438-1443.

Choy, E. (2017). *Let the story do the work: The art of storytelling for business success*. New York: AMACOM (now HarperCollins).

Clear, J. (n.d.). *First principles: Elon Musk on the power of thinking for yourself*. Retrieved from https://jamesclear.com/first-principles

Copy Hackers. (2018, March 13). *How to join the conversation happening in your customer's head*. Retrieved from https://copyhackers.com/join-the-conversation-customer/

Cranney, J., Ahn, M., McKinnon, R., Morris S., and Watts, K. (2009). The testing effect, collaborative learning, and retrieval-induced facilitation in a classroom setting. *European Journal of Cognitive Psychology*, *21*(6), 919-940. Retrieved from http://dx.doi.org/10.1080/09541440802413505

Dam, R., and Siang, T. (2018, December). What is design thinking and why is it so popular? *Interactive Design Foundation*. Retrieved from https://www.interaction-design.org/literature/article/what-is-design-thinking-and-why-is-it-so-popular

DraperTV. [Username]. (2015, January 28). *SpaceX and why they are daring to think big | Investor Steve Jurvetson* [Video File]. Retrieved from https://youtu.be/3aXNWGwis4w

Eagan, K., Stolzenberg, E.B., Lozano, J.B., Aragon, M.C., Suchard, M.R., and Hurtado, S. (2014). *Undergraduate teaching faculty: The 2013-2014 HERI faculty survey.* Los Angeles: Higher Education Research Institute, UCLA. Retrieved from https://www.heri.ucla.edu/monographs/HERI-FAC2014-monograph.pdf

Eng, N. (2017, December 10). *Reviewing for finals? Try affinity mapping* [web log]. Retrieved from https://normaneng.org/reviewing-for-finals-try-affinity-mapping/

Eng, N. (2018, April 23). *Introducing stop-jot-share* [web log]. Retrieved from https://normaneng.org/introducing-stop-jot-share/

Eng, N. (2018, September 24). Focus your lectures with the 'one-sentence lesson plan." *Faculty Focus.* Retrieved from https://www.facultyfocus.com/articles/teaching-and-learning/focus-your-lectures-with-the-one-sentence-lesson-plan/

Evergreen, S. (2017). *Presenting data effectively: Communicate your findings for maximum impact.* Newbury Park, CA: Sage Publications, Inc.

Godin, S. (n.d.). *Really bad PowerPoint (and how to avoid it)* [ebook]. Retrieved from http://www.sethgodin.com/freeprize/reallybad-1.pdf

Goodman, A. (2006). *Why bad presentations happen to good causes. And how to ensure they won't happen to yours.* Los Angeles, CA: Cause Communications.

Haile, T. (2014, March 9). What you think you know about the web is wrong. *Time.* Retrieved from http://time.com/12933/what-you-think-you-know-about-the-web-is-wrong/

Jaffe, J. (2009). *Join the conversation: How to engage marketing-weary consumers with the power of community, dialogue, and partnership.* Hoboken, NJ: Wiley.

Kahneman, D. (2013). *Thinking, fast and slow.* New York: Farrar, Straus, and Giroux.

Klaff, O. (2011). *Pitch anything: An innovative method for presenting, persuading, and winning the deal.* New York: McGraw Hill.

Krug, S. (2005). *Don't make me think: A common sense approach to web usability* (2nd ed). San Francisco, CA: New Riders.

Malek, M. [Username]. (2016, August 25). *Elon Musk first principle reasoning TED* [Video File]. Retrieved from https://youtu.be/0JQXoSmC1rs

Malmfors, B., Garnsworthy, P., Grossman, M. (2004). *Writing and presenting scientific papers*. Nottingham, UK: Nottingham University Press.

Mayer, R. E. (2009). *Multimedia learning* (2nd ed.). Cambridge, MA: Cambridge University Press.

McDermott, K.B., Agarwal, P.K., D'Antonio, L., Roediger, III, H.L., and McDaniel, M.A. (2014). *Journal of Experimental Psychology: Applied*. 20(1), 3-21. Retrieved from http://pdf.poojaagarwal.com/McDermott_etal_2014_JEPA.pdf

Meyers, C., and Jones, T. (1993). Promoting active learning: Strategies for the college classroom. San Francisco, CA: Jossey-Bass.

Middendorf, J., and Kalish, A. (1996). The "change-up" in lectures. *National Teaching and Learning Forum, 5*(2), 1–5.

Miller, G.E. (1962). An inquiry into medical teaching. *Journal of Medical Education, 37*(3), 185-191.

Nakano, C. (2016, June 16). Presentation habits presenters don't like to admit [web log post]. *Prezi* Blog. Retrieved from https://blog.prezi.com/presentation-habits-presenters-dont-like-to-admit/

Pauk, W. and Owens, R. (2013). *How to study in college* (11th ed.). Boston, MA: Cengage Learning.

Penner, J. (1984). *Why many college teachers cannot lecture.* Springfield, IL: Thomas.

Potter, M.C., Wyble, B., Hagmann, C.E., and McCourt, E.S. (2014). Detecting meaning in RSVP at 13 ms per picture. *Attention, Perception, & Psychophysics, 76*(2), 270-279. doi: 10.3758/s13414-013-0605-z

Snow, S. (2015, January 28). The surprising reading level analysis will change the way you write [web log post]. *Contently.* Retrieved from https://contently.com/2015/01/28/this-surprising-reading-level-analysis-will-change-the-way-you-write/

Stains, M., Harshman, J., Barker, M.K., Chasteen, S.V., Cole, R., DeChenne-Peters, S.E., Eagan, M.K., Esson, J.M., Knight, J.K., Laski, F.A., Levis-Fitzgerald, M., Lee, C.J., Lo, SM., McDonnell, L.M., McKay, T.A., Michelotti, N., Musgrove, A., Palmer, M.S., Plank, K.M., Rodela, T.M., Sanders, E.R., Schimpf, N.G., Schulte, P.M., Smith, M.K., Stetzer, M., Van Valkenburgh, B., Vinson, E., Weir, L.K., Wendel, P.J., Wheeler, L.B., Young, A.M. (2018). Anatomy of STEM teaching in North American universities. *Science, 359*(6383), 1468-1470.

Story, L. (2007, January 15). Anywhere the eye can see, it's likely to see an ad. *The New York Times.* Retrieved from https://www.nytimes.com/2007/01/15/business/media/15everywhere.html

Stuart, J., and Rutherford, R. (1978). Medical student concentration during lectures. *Lancet, 2,* 514-516.

Swaminathan, N. (2008). Why does the brain need so much power? *Scientific American.* Retrieved from https://www.scientificamerican.com/article/why-does-the-brain-need-s/

Watts, M., and Schaur, G. (2011). Teaching and assessment methods in undergraduate economics: A Fourth National Quinquennial Survey. *The Journal of Economic Education, 42*(3), 294–309.

Weissman, J. (2009). *Presenting to win: The art of telling your story* [updated and expanded edition]. Upper Saddle River, NJ: FT Press.

ABOUT THE AUTHOR

Norman Eng is a doctor of education (Ed.D.), with a background in teaching and marketing—two areas that relate to lecturing, presenting, and engaging audiences.

He is also the founder and president of EDUCATIONxDESIGN, Inc., which—through his books, coaching, consulting, and online course—helps professors amplify their work to influence the world.

Dr. Eng's book, *Teaching College: The Ultimate Guide to Lecturing, Presenting, and Engaging Students,* is widely read by faculty members and teachers everywhere. It consistently ranks #1 on Amazon's bestseller list in various education categories. Likewise, his online course, the *Teaching College Masterclass*, continues to help professors across the U.S. transform their lectures and lessons in the classroom.

IF YOU'RE PRESENTING, YOU'RE TEACHING.

FREE VIDEO TRAINING

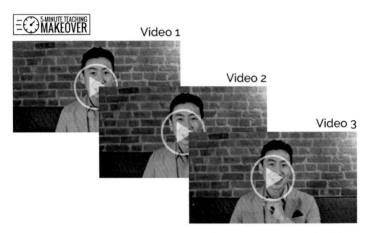

Get the insights that transform your teaching, including how to approach your lectures as well as my 5 recommendations that will captivate your students and 10X their learning.

In this FREE 3-part series, you'll learn:
- My #1 go-to lecture format that captivates students so they're siting on the edge of their seats.
- The 2 biggest myths professors believe about teaching that cause students to disengage (and how to avoid them)
- 5 recommendations to skyrocket student engagement starting with your next lecture.

Access your FREE training here:
NormanEng.org/5mtm

YOUR VOICE IS IMPORTANT

Did you find this book useful? Why or why not?
What worked particularly well for you?
What impact has this book had?
What do you wish could be addressed more?

Just tell me and I'll respond.

Norman@EducationXDesign.com

Made in United States
North Haven, CT
06 April 2024

50990226R00091